NIGEL

DO
MANAGE
LEAD

Essential Bible-based tools for leaders

WAVERLEY ABBEY
TRUST

Packed with rich illustrations, copious amounts of biblical wisdom and myriad insights from leaders in every sphere, Do Manage Lead had me gripped page after page. You may know several of the theories covered. Don't skip over! It was the Greek Aesop who said familiarity breeds contempt. For starters, Nigel reinvigorates the tired, often poorly executed SWOT, and sheds fresh light on Adair's Action Centred Leadership, and he goes on to highlight some you may be less familiar with, such as dealing with wicked problems and situational leadership. Theories tested by time, anchored in Scripture and weathered in real life. What's not to like? I will be recommending this to students!
Andy du Feu, Executive Director, Moorlands College

Brilliant book. Great mix of real world experiences grounded in scripture. I can see how I will apply this book to my leadership. This book will live in my office and I am very sure it will be opened a lot over the next few years. I only wish I had this toolbox when I started my leadership. I probably would have made wiser decisions.
Jon Partridge, CEO, RS Marine Group

Do Manage Lead is a fantastic resource. In looking at some common business theories and models for getting things done through the lens of scripture, Nigel expertly blends wisdom from well-known biblical narratives with insightful reflection. This book should be on every leaders shelf.
Ali Campbell, Development Consultant, Paraklesis

Nigel draws together what we now understand as essential business craft with practical and applicable biblical understanding. If the Bible is rightly understood as speaking to the whole of life and lived experience, why is that we fear to allow its light and truth to shine into the shrine of business?
Tammy Lillie BEng Hons MSc PGCLT(HE) CEng FIMechE FCIPD, Chief People Officer, Met Office

This book makes a distinctive and inspirational contribution to leadership and management resources. Nigel has skilfully woven together classic leadership and management theory with scriptural wisdom to create a highly effective toolkit for leaders. Leaders and managers, in a wide variety of contexts, would find this book of immense value as would those who coach and mentor existing or aspiring leaders. Anyone leading in a Church setting, particularly, would find the blend of leadership models and scriptural underpinnings both highly informative and inspirational. I would recommend this book wholeheartedly to all those engaged in improving the working lives of people and their organisations.
Dr Pat McGovern, Retired Headteacher, School Leadership Coach and Education Consultant.

What an encouragement to find a book that combines current secular models of leadership with a biblical interpretation. As a leader of a Christian Charity mainly served by teams of volunteers, it is refreshing to be able to reflect on the challenges of leadership and team building within a faith framework. Nigel provides us with some helpful passages from scripture along with some memorable stories from both his own

experience and others to illustrate the key points of each chapter. With punchy sections and short chapters, this book is very readable, and will provide a helpful addition to the resources available to support us in our different leadership positions. I particularly liked the 'And finally...' conclusion to each chapter, which succinctly brought the key themes together with a takeaway message. So, 'and finally' – I highly recommend this book to all those who are keen to both deepen their faith perspective of leadership, as well those who are looking for a useful toolbox to explore with their teams.
Revd Canon Dr Erica Roberts, Founder of Caraway, City Chaplain for Older People, Southampton

Nigel has the rare gift of taking complicated and occasionally dull but useful management and leadership principles and translating them into the church and charity world in a way that non-academics can understand. I am delighted that these tools, many of which have been shared with youth and children's workers will now have a wider audience. It is hard to imagine anyone reading these chapters and not finding an insight that will transform their service for God.
Andy Peck, editor of Youth and Children's Work and Premier NexGen.

This book is a great blend of good management practice and applied common sense, set in a valuable biblical perspective. It is well researched and referenced, and includes relevant examples from the Bible, and from the everyday life of organisations. *Do Manage Lead* will give you practical tools for dealing with a host of challenges and opportunities, whether you are a church leader, or a manager or Director or trustee of a Christian charity, or a Christian trying to live out your faith in a secular work environment.
David Saint, Chair, Action Planning Consultants

In *Do Manage Lead* Nigel Argall has set out to discuss some fourteen mainstream management theories and explain them in a straightforward manner as tools to make the leader's life easier. Although aimed primarily at a Christian readership, managers in a wide variety of professions will find his writing style engaging and his definitions and illustrations accessible. I thoroughly recommend this book as a step towards more skilled and effective leadership.
Roland Agambar, Managing Director, Mail Newspapers, DMG

I deeply appreciate this helpful book from an experienced and effective pastor who shares tried and true principles forged in the trenches of ministry. Drawing on both scripture and modern leadership tools, Pastor Argall offers a work that pastors will find both accessible and immanently practical.
Keith Cowart, Bishop, Free Methodist Church, USA

Do Manage Lead offers a creative, insightful, accessible, and practical toolkit for Christians at all levels of leadership or management – even if you're just managing yourself! A highly refreshing approach that incorporates a healthy dialogue between Biblical reflection, faith, real-life scenarios, and a range of practical management theories.
Revd Louise Kenyon, Lecturer in Social Theology, Nazarene Theological College, Manchester

This is a beautifully balanced guide - an entertaining and purposeful walk through clearly articulated ideas, with a usefully wide range of cultural and theoretical reference. Nigel's writing comes from a wealth of practical experience, and his constant re-reference to Scripture gives the narrative a solid biblical framework.
Professor Timothy Dean, Royal Conservatoire of Scotland

Through stories, scriptures and helpful strategies Nigel offers us tools that equip us in the leadership journey and always tracks us back to the Bible. An essential read that will encourage any leader.
Amy Summerfield CEO, Kyria Network, Head of Development, Skylark International, Zeo Church

Nigel has created a concise 'toolbox' that equips and encourages us to tackle difficult challenges all too easily filed in the 'too difficult basket', and succeed. Being rooted in God's word, perhaps the only prescription he puts forward is to 'seek and ye shall find'.
Phil Rice, Chief Financial Officer, Falmouth University

As beings 'made in the image of God', we should not be surprised that many of our experiences in life are reflected in God's dealings with His people as recorded in the Bible. This book astutely makes use of scripture to identify key tools to help those with responsibility or leadership, in any walk of life, to have the confidence to navigate life's issues and dramas.
Lt Col (Ret'd) Bill Graham, British Army

Nigel shares honest insights from the wealth of his, and others', experiences. Applying these principles will enlarge our leadership toolkit and increase our skill level. Well worth a read.
John Townley National Leader, Free Methodist Church, UK and Ireland

Love this and really appreciate what you've written.
Sarah Yardley, Mission and Ministry lead, Creationfest

ACKNOWLEDGEMENTS

Bob Stradling, Principal of Waverley Abbey College, had a huge input into this book. We come from similar backgrounds, fascinated by the intersection of theology and management/leadership theory. Bob expressed an interest in the project at an early stage and was incredibly generous with his time and wisdom over a long series of Zoom meetings where we discussed the contents of each chapter. 'As iron sharpens iron, so one person sharpens another' (Prov. 27:17), and Bob was the very sharp but constructively critical friend any author needs, despite the numerous claims on his time and energy. Many of the best insights and stories are his. For cock-ups, errors, omissions and inaccuracies, I take full responsibility.

I am also grateful to Premier Media Group. Ruth Jackson (then Editor of *Youth and Children's Work* magazine) gave me the chance to write for them a number of years ago and the material in my 'Toolbox' column has provided the basis for the thinking foundational to this book.

Thanks also to Jax Machin, priest and psychotherapist extraordinaire.

To the team at Waverley Abbey Trust, thanks for believing in this book and making it happen. I am particularly grateful to Rebecca Berry for her excellent editorial guidance.

For Helen, my best friend on the journey.

CONTENTS

FOREWORD

Most of us will have worked with brilliant leaders, and in dynamic and fulfilling teams. Yet you will, no doubt, have also been frustrated by the opposite, with ineffective teams and uninspiring and demotivating leaders, even though the people were skilled, committed and worthy. Let's be honest, this probably happens at least as often in church as in secular employment. In this book, Nigel Argall asks whether in these situations Christians can benefit from established models of management and leadership? Is secular leadership something different to that in a church, or do these require different models and styles? Can Christians use the skills that they have learnt at work and join the dots to see how these can be used to reflect essential characteristics of Christian vocation, service and behaviour? Nigel asks if we are happy to draw on sources of wisdom from authors and practitioners who may not share our faith perspective, but still have insights and wisdom to share? He answers this question with a clear 'yes'.

In this short book, Nigel Argall outlines some of the major secular management and leadership tools that have been developed over the years, and he uses bible stories to show how these principles have been applied by people of God. These are illustrated with examples from his own wide experience in different contexts. There is no secular-spiritual divide here, the same wise principles apply in both church and secular contexts. Nigel is bold to acknowledge this and does not duck the conclusion that while personal integrity and commitment are essential requirements for Christian leadership, these alone are not sufficient for effective leadership. He emphasises that these skills can be learned, developed and enhanced. Readers of the book will be relieved to know that he doesn't indulge in deep analysis and description of the various tools, but provides clear and succinct summaries of their main conclusions. Neither is this a book of quick-fix formulae, but by raising the issues Nigel provokes us to consider how we can use these tools to improve our own situations.

I recommend this book as a starting point, to set you thinking about how things might operate better.

Keith Fox is Emeritus Professor of Biochemistry at Southampton University where he was for a time Head of the School of Biological Sciences. He was Associate Director and then Director of the Faraday Institute for Science and Religion in Cambridge and was a former chair of Christians in Science. He was Senior Executive Editor of a major academic science journal (Nucleic Acids Research) from 2008-2021 and is Editor of Science & Christian Belief. He is also a Licensed Lay Minister in the Church of England.

INTRODUCTION

Start here.

Imagine: You get a new electronic device and open the box. Out comes the device, charger, and way too much packaging. You also get an instruction manual that is 300 pages thick and in ten different languages. Mercifully, you also find the 'quick-start guide' that gets you up and going in two minutes. All the basics are there on one side of A5. Usually (say, five years later), you find the manual in a drawer and realise it has lasted longer than the device.

I like short books.

This chapter is your quick-start guide – it may run to a few pages, but it will help you get a feel for where we are going and what to expect. Overall, I hope this book will in turn be a quick-start guide to life – a shortcut to some brilliant insights.

In *The Road Less Travelled*, M. Scott Peck says, 'Life is difficult. This is a great truth, one of the greatest truths. It is a great truth because once we truly see this truth, we transcend it... once it is accepted, the fact that life is difficult no longer matters.'[1] This book is about making life – our work, management and leading – just a little less difficult (because life really can be difficult).

Western cultures in particular seem to revere and value knowledge ('Knowledge is power', said Francis Bacon, c1597) but don't value wisdom. Perhaps because of the value of knowledge, we are generally not very good at sharing 'wisdom' in our culture. Why should we? It would be like giving away cash. In recent years I have managed to make part of my living as a coach and mentor. I have lost count of how many times I have grabbed a table menu in a coffee shop and sketched something on it to help someone through a situation. People pay me for this! So my aim in writing this book is to share with you some of that wisdom, in the hope that it will empower you to step up your own leadership practices.

I really believe that these tools will help you unlock situations and make sense of what is happening, give you confidence, and help you navigate your way through tough decisions when they come.

Before we devour all the management and leadership advice that's out there, there's another something else to consider: As a Christian, do I *agree* with these theories? How do these theories relate to scripture and my faith?

Let's think about this in a different scenario. If you were feeling unwell with an undiagnosed malady, would you: a) pray about it; b) go to the doctor; or c) pray about it *and* go to the doctor? It's not meant to be a trick question – even though there isn't really a right answer. While it might be lovely to have a doctor who shares your faith, most of us wouldn't deem that essential – mostly, if the doctor can cure us using modern medicine, we go away happy. Now reflect on the life you live, or the work and ministry you do. Are you happy to draw on sources of wisdom from authors and practitioners who may not share your faith perspective on the world, but still have some insight or wisdom to share? I believe that with an intelligent and cautious approach, we can draw from a huge range of theories to enhance and empower our lives.

I love making things: over the years I have pretty much built a conservatory, a loft conversion, and several surf boards. For this I have needed a whole range of tools. Some I use all the time; some are a bit specialised and only come out for unusual applications. Some are, to be honest, so specialised I hardly ever use them, so I will either hire or borrow them. I use the tool and then put it away (or return it to its owner). But the point is, these tools are at my disposal, and they each have a purpose for which to be used.

All of us at some point will face tasks and difficulties, and times when we're trying to make sense of a situation. Frequently the questions will be prompted by disappointment: 'We planned, we prayed... and it still didn't work – what happened?' If I were to summarise this book using one Bible verse, it would be Psalm 78:72: 'And David shepherded them with integrity of heart; with skilful hands he led them.' It's not heart *or* hands – we need both. This book is focused a little more on the 'skilful hands'.

What's in your toolbox?

As human beings, we have acquired a huge range of tools that can give us insights and explanations as to what is going on under the surface of the behaviour we observe. Reflecting on my own 35 years in ministry (and counting), I think I probably use about a dozen separate theories to help me make sense of situations I find myself in. Most of these are not specifically Christian, although one or two were invented by Christians.

The great educational theorist Abraham Maslow famously said, 'It is tempting, if the only tool you have is a hammer, to treat everything as if it is a nail.'[2] I have noticed that most of us living and working in any professional capacity start to accumulate a set of tools as life progresses – just like a master craftsman, getting familiar with your favourite tools, knowing when to apply them, which tool is most appropriate and the limits and weaknesses of each, is itself a major part of the skill. Getting the right tools is important. A hundred years before Maslow, factory workers would refer to a 'Birmingham screwdriver', which was really a hammer. A critical engineer might say, 'Wow, this has been put together with a Birmingham screwdriver.' This tendency to only use what we have is so prevalent, it has its own name: The Law of Instrument. Take, for example, a young person with an eating disorder. A doctor will see it as a medical problem, a psychiatrist as a mental health issue, and a sociologist as an example of a social phenomenon especially prevalent in young people, and a teacher will see it as something impacting a student's education. None are wrong, but each is reverting to the clinical perspective inherent in their background and training. The joy of having more tools in your box is the ability to choose what explains things best.

Having spoken to hundreds of professionals over the years (both in Christian ministry and secular employment), I think most people will adopt and use eight to ten mainstream management tools on a regular basis. Your choice will depend on your context but will have a personal component – some tools will simply resonate with your way of thinking so that you will have a natural knack in adopting and using them. This is normal, and totally OK – like the guy with the Birmingham screwdriver, don't force something that does not work for you.

Remember: theoretical tools, like real tools, can cause destruction and injury when misused! So I'd like to propose a few 'safety principles' for us to bear in mind before we go on:

- Tools are always a simplification; an abstract way of looking at what is actually pretty complex and messy human behaviour. Don't expect too much – like a metaphor, these explanations and insights will always eventually break down. These limits do not, however, devalue the key insight the tool brings.

- The best tools are very simple. This gives them the weakness noted above (they don't explain everything) but, crucially, simplicity makes them easier to remember and apply. Complex theories might be more accurate but are harder to remember and use. Like a bear of little brain, I like simple tools.

- The best tools will give you that 'Ah-ha!' moment where you suddenly manage to make sense of a situation for the first time.

- Although some of these approaches may connect ins some ways, don't try to cross reference from one tool to another – try to use just one at a time. Use the theory to understand what is going on, take the insight, and then put it away in the toolbox. To stick with our metaphor, fretsaws and bows saws are both saws, but serve very different purposes. Fretsaws do delicate stuff and bowsaws are good at cutting tree branches. (We are going to break this rule in the very last chapter, but you'll have to wait for that!)

- Remember that the tool is there to serve you, not the other way around. When you carry management or leadership responsibility, you have power in people's lives. When people work with or for us, they give us a part of their life. This is an incredible responsibility. These tools are here to help you get this awesome responsibility right.

I can almost guarantee that you will already be using at least one of these tools. It may be that you are already familiar with specific approaches, but it may also be that you are instinctively thinking along these lines. People often have a partial understanding of a tool. Lots of people use the phrase 'win-win', for example (see chapter 1) but seldom explore the other options. It may be that you are using these tools without knowing it, but it is helpful to know *why it works* – you didn't know that you knew it until someone told you that you did! An explicit understanding of the tool enables you to wield it better, master its intricacies, acknowledge its limits, and gain confidence in using it.

Faith

Central to everything is a bit of basic but superimportant theology that underpins everything in this book. I believe first that we are made in the image of God. The doctrine of *Imago Dei* does not allow us to confer human qualities onto our image of God, but the reverse: it is a belief that we have that imprint of God (and I mean all of us), and are therefore capable of God-like things such as love, creativity, mercy, compassion, rationality, morality, and self-sacrifice. History is littered with tyrants who loved their wives and children, and had artistic and creative skills. I believe we are sinners – all of us carry the brokenness of that 'God image' within us – we are less than we were created to be and fail at many things. Being a Christian should make us more human, not less; more connected to people, not divided. Many non-Christians have produced wonderful and helpful work which is both creative and insightful, because it is impossible to eradicate that image of God within them, even if they do not personally acknowledge it. So, tools authored by people who do not share your faith perspective of the world, can be used if they are consistent with scripture – but not if not.

A few years ago, I did a master's degree in Community Education with a strong emphasis on equal opportunities and anti-oppressive practice. Some of the writers we studied had good insights but were convinced that people were intrinsically 'good', and any negative behaviour was explained by the oppressions that they suffer. I simply can't agree with this. I do believe people are created in the image of God and are wonderful. I also hold in tension a belief that we are all sinners – that image is marred and broken. I can debate with but not agree with a theorist who can't see the sinful side of humans. This also means that if I am right, we will see these theories being lived out in the stories of God's people in scripture.

Recalling a fiery debate with one of his own lecturers at university, Archbishop Stephen Cottrell put this rather well: '[Your] assumption is that everybody's good and they will do good things, and my assumption is not that everyone is bad, but that actually the human heart is a rebel – we have an inbuilt tendency to put ourselves first and exclude others. Dare I say it, we are sinners in need of repentance.'[3] The prophet Jeremiah put it even more succinctly: 'The heart is deceitful above all things' (Jer. 17:9).

I was recently in conversation with the global vice-president of a multi-billion-dollar and fast-growing IT company, who said: 'I can be a Christian at work, but it is hard to take my faith to work – I can't use it directly in explaining the decisions I make. At times it feels like I live in two worlds – the world of work and my world of faith. Sometimes it seems that there is nothing bridging these two worlds and if anything, they are growing farther apart.' I like to think of this book as an attempt to bridge those two worlds, to show the hidden threads of God's creativity at work in all of us – whether we know Him or are still searching.

Do, Manage, Lead is not about mixing a bit of this and that. We are really going to engage with theories as they were originally conceived. I'm going to point out weaknesses as well as strengths, and critique them with as much honesty and integrity as I can.

In his book *The Enneagram: A Christian Perspective*[4] (about a personality typology you may want to explore further), Richard Rohr notes the Christian tendency to 'baptise' ideas and models into a faith context. An early example might be Paul in Athens claiming the 'Unknown God' as Yahweh (Acts 17). Despite the validity of this tradition, that is not what we are doing here. We will take each tool seriously and be honest about how well it resonates with Christian thinking.

What's in the book?

The book is structured into three parts, as you may have guessed:
Do; Manage; Lead.

Management guru Peter Drucker is widely quoted as saying
'Management is doing things right; leadership is doing the right
things.'[5] It has become accepted in modern leadership thinking to
acknowledge that most of us spend time 'doing' (ploughing through
spreadsheets, devising rotas), some time 'managing' (making sure stuff
actually happens safely, well and on time), and are sometimes 'leading'
(the big picture, strategic planning, and development activities). The
reality is that in any day, most of us will seamlessly transition between
all three functions. We are going to cover all three key areas looking at
mainstream thinking. Incidentally, I have deliberately chosen theories
which have gained traction and are widely known – they may not be
the most cutting edge ideas but they do follow the thinking that you are
most likely to encounter in your professional life.

Each chapter also follows a pattern. We will start to explore each issue
and find examples in scripture. We will then get our heads around the
theory or tool, before returning to those Bible passages to see how it
works out in those narratives, and also in life.

There is an important caveat here. I believe that we *can* see these
tools being worked out in scripture – the danger is that we take scripture
and impose our meaning on to it. In many cases we will see certain parts
of a theory being worked out in one passage, and the rest of it in a later
section. Scripture is a light to our path, not a convenient handbook to
prove our points.

'Ah-ha!' moments

Just over a hundred years ago, my grandfather went to the trenches
in the First World War. He survived but the experienced scarred him
forever – you might say it shaped his outlook, values, and politics for
the rest of his 101-year life. In those days there was no name for post-

traumatic stress disorder. Psychiatrists were just beginning to use the crude expression of 'shell shock' to try to make sense of those who were perhaps physically uninjured, but nevertheless traumatised by their experiences. Linguistic relativity hypothesis tells us that we need words to be able to process things; we don't simply understand in an abstract way. Our thoughts are constructed and embedded in a specific language. As Desmond Tutu said, 'Language is very powerful. Language does not just describe reality. Language creates the reality it describes.'[6] The theories in this book are a way of enabling us to articulate and explore situations – giving us the language, if you like. Situations may not be negotiable, but they can be navigated if we can understand them. John O'Donohue puts this rather beautifully in his book *Anam Cara*: 'Each day our tribe of language holds what we call the 'world' together... everyone is an artist. Each person brings sound out of the silence and coaxes the invisible to become visible.'[7] I love that metaphor, and it helps explain the 'Ah-ha!' moments. What was perceptible has, in a way, suddenly been made visible. We can see what is actually going on and perhaps also what we need to do in response.

So, what follows is a range of the most popular and best loved tools. Remember that this is a 'toolbox', so you don't have to work through them sequentially, but pick and choose for each challenge. Inevitably, there is an element of personal choice – in the ones I have explored here and the ones you will get to like. I really pray that what you are holding in your hands is going to unlock some amazing and creative insights for you. Enjoy!

DO

CHAPTER 1:
WINNERS AND LOSERS

Here's my strategy on the Cold War:
we win, they lose.

Ronald Reagan, 40th US President[1]

This tool has nothing to do with the sorts of motivational talks that coaches give in the changing room at half time. Win-win is much more a way of looking at all the interpersonal relationships we have in life, work, business, and ministry, and thinking about who benefits.

To get the full insight, I recommend Stephen Covey's book, *The 7 Habits of Highly Effective People.*[2] Covey would be the first to admit that he did not invent this 'win-win' approach, but he most definitely popularised it and brought it into mainstream culture. It's worth noting that, just like many of the theories we'll be considering, its familiarity to us often results in sloppy thinking. I've lost count of the number of times people have declared, 'It's a win-win!' Sometimes it is, sometimes it's not so clear – and we seldom explore the importance of the alternatives.

Bible stories

Unless you work in sales, the whole issue of negotiating deals (or what we might call 'haggling') might be a bit alien to you. You might dip in and out of this activity very occasionally (buying a car, a house, negotiating a pay rise), but it is likely not a significant part of your everyday life. Most supermarkets will not respond well to your persuasive bid for a massive discount on food or petrol. For some cultures however, both past and present, haggling is a way of life and a major part of the fun of shopping. For these reasons, it may take a little effort of the imagination to get our heads around the Bible stories we'll be referring to in this chapter – especially when we remember that the two stories here take place between 2,500 and 4,000 years ago, when women were used as bargaining chips. Some of the gendered cultural values may seem deeply offensive to us today, but were widely practised at the time.

Genesis 29:14–28

After Jacob had stayed with him for a whole month, Laban said to him, 'Just because you are a relative of mine, should you work for me for nothing? Tell me what your wages should be.'

Now Laban had two daughters; the name of the older was Leah, and the name of the younger was Rachel. Leah had weak eyes, but Rachel had a lovely figure and was beautiful. Jacob was in love with Rachel and said, 'I'll work for you seven years in return for your younger daughter Rachel.'

Laban said, 'It's better that I give her to you than to some other man. Stay here with me.' So Jacob served seven years to get Rachel, but they seemed like only a few days to him because of his love for her. Then Jacob said to Laban, 'Give me my wife. My time is completed, and I want to make love to her.' So Laban brought together all the people of the place and gave a feast. But when evening came, he took his daughter Leah and brought her to Jacob, and Jacob made love to her. And Laban gave his servant Zilpah to his daughter as her attendant. When morning came, there was Leah! So Jacob said to Laban, 'What is this you have done to me? I served you for Rachel, didn't I? Why have you deceived me?' Laban replied, 'It is not our custom here to give the younger daughter in marriage before the older one. Finish this daughter's bridal week; then we will give you the younger one also, in return for another seven years of work.' And Jacob did so.

Jacob and Laban are old-school hagglers. Jacob himself is one of the truly enigmatic characters of the Old Testament. His first real encounter with God is in Genesis 28, right after deceiving his father into blessing him, and even here, he can't help driving a deal. Notice that his commitment to God is conditional ('*If* God will be with me...'), and he can't help offering God a 10% commission on what is His already. Jacob and Laban's efforts to negotiate and outwit each other border on the comic. They are tied together by family links and custom but still set out to get the better of each other while just about staying within the rules. Whilst this is clearly offensive to our twenty-first century thinking, the reality was that women were largely seen as the property of either their father or husband. Jacob manages to dangerously mix business with emotion by falling for Laban's daughter Rachel, and Laban sets out to amplify his benefit, leveraging this deal to the max.

2 Samuel 3:6–16

During the war between the house of Saul and the house of David, Abner had been strengthening his own position in the house of Saul. Now Saul had had a concubine named Rizpah daughter of Aiah. And Ish-Bosheth said to Abner, 'Why did you sleep with my father's concubine?'

Abner was very angry because of what Ish-Bosheth said. So he answered, 'Am I a dog's head – on Judah's side? This very day I am loyal to the house of your father Saul and to his family and friends. I haven't handed you over to David. Yet now you accuse me of an offense involving this woman! May God deal with Abner, be it ever so severely, if I do not do for David what the LORD promised him on oath and transfer the kingdom from the house of Saul and establish David's throne over Israel and Judah from Dan to Beersheba.' Ish-Bosheth did not dare to say another word to Abner, because he was afraid of him. Then Abner sent messengers on his behalf to say to David, 'Whose land is it? Make an agreement with me, and I will help you bring all Israel over to you.'

'Good,' said David. 'I will make an agreement with you. But I demand one thing of you: Do not come into my presence unless you bring Michal daughter of Saul when you come to see me.' Then David sent messengers to Ish-Bosheth son of Saul, demanding, 'Give me my wife Michal, whom I betrothed to myself for the price of a hundred Philistine foreskins.'

So Ish-Bosheth gave orders and had her taken away from her husband

Paltiel son of Laish. Her husband, however, went with her, weeping behind her all the way to Bahurim. Then Abner said to him, 'Go back home!' So he went back.

Stories of David are the staple of any Sunday school. Who hasn't heard of David and Goliath? The truth, however, is that as well as the stories of heroism, there is a whole lot of rough, political bargaining as well. This narrative is full of detail and cultural allusion. Abner is clearly sensing that whilst Saul's son Ish-Bosheth is the new king, David's star is in the ascendency whilst the dynasty of Saul is on the wane. The accusation by Ish-Bosheth that Abner might have slept with one of his father's concubines is highly significant. Concubines were considered to be a significant personal possession, and to sleep with one belonging to a king was not just discourteous but seen as an attack on the king – effectively insulting the crown and indicating that indeed, the king's power (or in this case, that of his successor) was ineffective. Abner makes a show of loyalty (verse 9 is effectively an oath of self-inflicted curse), but this appears to be the tipping point where his allegiance switches to David. Abner contacts David. This is an incredible moment and potentially huge coup for David, but how will he handle the negotiation?

The theory

Covey's argument is that in any human negotiation (say for example, I'm asking you to volunteer to join my team or do a tricky piece of work), there are four possible outcomes:

- Lose-win

- Lose-lose

- Win-lose

- Win-win

Covey later added two more possibilities: 'win', where winning is all that matters, and 'no deal', where two individuals or organisations recognise that their values and intentions are so diverse, it is simply better to walk away from a potential deal. Most thinking, however, has been done on the four traditional options and we are going to mostly consider these.

In each case, the first word describes how I come out of the transaction and the second describes your outcome. To understand this, let's take a real-life example.

A UK-based Christian college owned a magnificent country house which had been purchased by its original founder. The house provided a genuinely beautiful and peaceful location for its educational activities but also had all the expense and liabilities which go with maintaining a large and very old country residence. It also had grounds which were, frankly, too big. They were underused but still relatively expensive to maintain. Meanwhile, an expanding Christian prayer ministry initiative was looking for a new HQ. It had outgrown its current location (based in a church) and needed somewhere that could be both a centre for its activities, training, and potentially large 'festival' type events. There was clearly some congruence and overlap with the needs of the college but also differences. Could something creative and helpful to both sides be achieved?

Negotiations commenced and resulted in a bold plan. A proposal was made that the ministry would purchase the house, solving their need for accommodation and a venue for large events at one stroke. The college would then lease back the classroom accommodation when it was needed for courses, enabling it to massively reduce its overheads and costs whilst still having access to the classrooms and accommodation that it needed.

This sounds like a story with a happy ending, and it was – but that masks the possibility and risk of it going badly wrong. Possible scenarios were:

Win-lose: The college is less than candid regarding the maintenance needs of the building they are selling and the real costs of keeping up the grounds. The ministry find they have saddled themselves with a ruinously expensive, if grand, location. The college wins, the ministry loses; it's a win-lose.

Lose-win: The college does the deal but effectively ends up being exploited by their new landlords with rental price hikes, little co-operation on booking and deliberately poor access to the space they need, whilst the ministry clearly prioritises its own activities. It's lose-win.

Lose-lose: The negotiating process breaks down over misunderstandings. Both sides have already incurred solicitors' costs, expensive surveys, and a need to temporarily find other accommodation. The relationship deteriorates further until both sides are actively pursuing the other for compensation. All the funds are lost in legal fees. It's a lose-lose.

Win-win: Both sides are assiduously honest. A fair price and process is negotiated and both sides aid the other in what are huge logistical changes. Their working relationship is strengthened, and a strong future partnership established. It's a win-win.

It's easy to see in this example just how complex creating a win-win scenario might be. It is hard enough in a simple transaction but the capacity for misunderstanding in a complex business negotiation is, of course, enormous. Win-win needs to be prized, valued, and intentionally sought after. As always, there may be personality aspects here; some people may take a loss in order to avoid conflict. You may even want to find ways (when negotiating) of asking, 'Are you happy with what you are getting out of this?'

We are often encouraged by the society we live in to think win-lose – if I can get one over on you, I have succeeded. We believe we only truly win if the other person loses. Think about this for a moment. In the short term I may 'win', but in the long term our relationship will suffer. Worse, you may tell your friends, colleagues, and professional business partners and my reputation suffers – no-one wants to work with me or have anything to do with me. In light of this, it's always worth considering whether 'winning' in the short-term may actually mean losing in the long-term – and vice versa.

Equally, we all know what it feels like to be on the receiving end of a lose-win transaction – to realise that we have in some way been conned into doing something. The other party has got what they wanted but we are left feeling used and undervalued. Lose-lose scenarios may sound rare, but they do happen – very often when both sides are angry and frustrated. The old phrase 'to cut off your nose to spite your face' sums up nicely both the futility and destructiveness of a lose-lose scenario.

Students of Old Testament theology will know that the word we tend to translate as 'peace', *shalom*, has a much richer and broader meaning in its original context. *Shalom* encompasses seven aspects, namely peace, harmony, wholeness, completeness, prosperity, welfare, and tranquillity. *Shalom* is impossible in anything other than a win-win context. I cannot have *shalom* if I have won but you have lost. *Shalom* challenges us to consider the other side of any deal.

Incidentally, one of the unique aspects of working as a Christian is that we will sometimes find ourselves leading, managing, and working with volunteers. Managing volunteers is a subject in its own right, but I want to suggest that win-win thinking is vital to success in this slightly specialised context. For example:

1. As a church-based youth worker, I would occasionally be phoned by another youth worker to see if I would be the 'guest speaker' at their residential – flattering, but also a pretty big ask, requiring a lot of my time, energy, and preparation. Thinking win-win, I could say something like, 'OK, yes... but I've got a couple of older teenagers who I'm training and mentoring – can I bring them along so they can maybe do a talk or two and get some experience?' Note how it is me who makes this a win-win – I get a brilliant discipling opportunity for some of my young people and the other guy gets his guest speaker for the residential.

2. The local school resists all offers of Christian assemblies. Thinking win-win, I want to build a mutually beneficial relationship with them and

eventually find that they'd love me to do a small project with children at risk of exclusion. I get a foothold in the school and a chance to build trust, and they get help with vulnerable children. Both sides win.

It is also worth noting that there are several relatively rare occasions when options other than win-win are OK – in sport, for example. Most parents will know the feeling of diving the wrong way in the football game with their young child just to let them win. It's a fact that if I win a sporting match, my opponent loses. We all know this and the pain of losing makes the taste of victory even more sweet. Sport simply can't work with an 'all must have prizes' approach. I had to win the heart of my wife several years ago, before she would marry me. So, for those of you who fancied her, tough – I won the girl.

Despite saying 'psychological analysis of Jesus is not appropriate',[3] theologian and author David Augsburger uses the language of win-win, or in these cases, win-lose. In both the cleansing of the temple (Mark 11:11–19) and the 'woe' monologue against the pharisees (Matthew 23), Jesus is happy to take a win-lose result without compromise. There are occasions when something other than win-win is what we settle for but, mostly... win-win is the aim.

Back to scripture

Interestingly, Covey was a God-fearing man (although not specifically Christian), which is perhaps why much of his thinking has a generous and loving core verging on the spiritual. Win-win works not because it is somehow spiritual, but because it is about how humans (made in the image of God) should be. There is much in the Old Testament wisdom literature and law about honesty, and the fundamental importance of being fair and straightforward in our dealings with people.

So, how do Jacob and Laban handle their negotiation?

Genesis 29:28–30

And Jacob did so. He finished the week with Leah, and then Laban gave
him his daughter Rachel to be his wife. Laban gave his servant Bilhah to
his daughter Rachel as her attendant. Jacob made love to Rachel also,
and his love for Rachel was greater than his love for Leah. And he worked
for Laban another seven years.

This turns out to be quite a complex negotiation. Jacob works for
nothing for a month. This might look like lose-win for Jacob but clearly,
he is building relationship and trust with his employer. Then Laban says,
'Tell me what your wages should be'. Despite the advantage of Jacob's
free labour, there is a cultural imperative here – and indeed a whole
raft of possibly hidden cultural issues. In saying, 'You are my own flesh
and blood' (v14), Laban implies that he may adopt Jacob as a son. If
so, instead of the implications of sonship (including inheritance), Laban
twists the situation into Jacob becoming a hired hand. Jacob is effectively
a relative, and only slaves worked for 'free'. Sensing his real value, and
his love for Rachel, Jacob negotiates for Rachel's hand in marriage in
exchange for seven years labour. This ostensibly looks like some sort of a
win-win, but the twist is that Laban palms off the elder daughter Leah on
him, making it most definitely a lose-win on the wedding day. Laban gets
his eldest daughter married, but Jacob does not get what he bargained
for: despite doing the work agreed, Laban callously doubles his terms.

Students of the Old Testament will know that this far from the end of
the story. Many years later (see Genesis 30), Jacob makes a first attempt
to escape from Laban. Laban has recognised by now how much of his
own wealth has been created by Jacob and resists ('Name your wages,
and I will pay them', v28). Jacob has learned at the feet of a master and
stays long enough to thwart Laban's attempts to genetically engineer his
adoption of the best of the flocks of sheep and goats. By now tensions
are rising: Laban's own sons are clearly recognising a threat to their own
inheritance and with masterful understatement the narrative says, 'Jacob
noticed that Laban's attitude towards him was not what it had been'. By
chapter 31, a messy and fearful split has been negotiated.

2 Samuel 3:17–18

Abner conferred with the elders of Israel and said, 'For some time you have wanted to make David your king. Now do it! For the LORD promised David, "By my servant David I will rescue my people Israel from the hand of the Philistines and from the hand of all their enemies."'

Just as there was cultural significance in the alleged defilement of Saul's concubine, there is huge import in David getting his wife back. Michal had been promised to David by Saul but then lost to him when he fled Saul's household. Any compassion that David might have had for Michal's new husband seems to have been trumped by the symbolic value of him winning her back from the house of Saul. Despite the bleakness of the bargaining, it is an example of win-win for David and Abner (though in Abner's case, the benefit is short-lived with a revenge killing in the same chapter).

And finally…

Whilst we are culturally encouraged to think win-lose, there is huge historical evidence that 'losers' will not want to stay that way. Short-term success too often turns into long-term loss. Germany lost the First World War but, in the big picture of history, there is a strong argument that the punitive terms of the Treaty of Versailles (a win-lose for the allies) ultimately led to the rise of National Socialism as a political force in Germany, and subsequently the Second World War.

In Matthew 26:14–16, Judas does the most awful deal in history by agreeing to betray Jesus' location and identity to His enemies in return for 30 pieces of silver. In the short term this is a win-win – both sides got what they wanted – but it does lead into a final thought.

I'm a huge fan of win-win thinking. I use it at work, church and in my family. It's an incredibly positive, life-affirming way of making agreements. However, like all concepts, it has its limits. Thinking win-win may be a clear and analytical way of looking at a situation, but life may also have other rich and complex dimensions. Win-win may be useful, but it may not be *enough*. Some things simply shouldn't be up for negotiation. They are too precious, or have already been agreed in a promise or commitment that should not be broken. But for everything else... think win-win!

CHAPTER 2:
CONFLICT, WHAT CONFLICT?

> *Conflict of itself is neither good nor bad, right*
> *nor wrong. It simply is. How we view, approach*
> *and work through our differences does – to a*
> *large extent – determine our whole life pattern.*
>
> **David Augsburger,** *Caring Enough to Confront*[1]

Conflict?! We don't really *do* conflict as Christians – I mean, never mind loving each other, we are called to love even our enemies. But the reality is, we do 'do conflict' more often than we might think and anyone who has lived through the pain of conflict on a team, a church split, or the breakdown of a Christian organisation knows what we are talking about. Many of us may work in secular environments where the approach to conflict may be much more open and occasionally even brutal.

Any Christian cultural assumption that we can live happily ever after in harmony is patently ridiculous. Jesus said in Luke 12:51, 'Do you think I came to bring peace on earth? No, I tell you, but division.' I love the phrase in 2 Samuel 11: 'In the spring, when Kings go out to war...' (v1). Note the 'when', not 'if'. War was so normal it was scheduled into the year.

Most of us tend to avoid conflict, but it is not all bad. Many of us will, for example, have had the experience of being on a team where one member does not pull their weight. Worse still, the team leader has perhaps refused to really tackle this. Conflict can clear the air and bring resolution to situations that have been simmering for a long time. I have only once fallen out badly with a boss. I'd describe the eventual altercation as a 'stand-up row' except for the fact that we were both sitting either side of a desk. The experience was incredibly stressful but also exhilarating. I remember driving home flooded with adrenaline but thinking, 'At last – it's out in the open – I've been able to say all the things I have wanted to say for years!'

One of my favourite conflict stories from the corporate world is that of the Dassler brothers, Adolf and Rudolf, founders of global brands Adidas and Puma. They had worked together as shoe manufacturers in the German town of Herzogenaurach for nearly 30 years from the company's foundation in 1919 until 1948. Different theories account for their falling out, but what is known is that their sudden conflict was dramatic, personal, and corporate. Adolf developed the company into Adidas (known for their product development and innovation), whilst Rudolf set up Puma with a more aggressive focus on sales. The town was itself split with clearly defined workforces in the rival factories. Legend has it that on meeting someone in Herzogenaurach, you would look first at their feet to see which brand of shoe they were wearing and therefore which 'tribe' they belonged to. The two workforces employed someone from almost every family in the town and patronised different bars, bakeries, and shops – something that was facilitated by the river that ran through the centre of town, itself dividing the two factories.

The companies went on to sponsor rival football teams and competing athletes, often using bitter tactics to outwit the other company. Rudolf and Adolf were never publicly reconciled and died within four years of each other in the 1970s. They are buried at opposite ends of the cemetery in Herzogenaurach.

Conflict is not all bad, and in most cases it won't be that extreme – but it can be destructive. How do we handle it well?

Bible stories

Acts 15:1–2

Certain people came down from Judea to Antioch and were teaching the believers: 'Unless you are circumcised, according to the custom taught by

Moses, you cannot be saved.' This brought Paul and Barnabas into sharp dispute and debate with them. So Paul and Barnabas were appointed, along with some other believers, to go up to Jerusalem to see the apostles and elders about this question.

This is a classic conflict. Ostensibly it is about the religious ritual of male circumcision, and its roots lay in the histories of the two strands of the emerging church – those from a Jewish background with its emphasis on ritual observance, and those converted Gentiles who had no such baggage. What might seem a minor point of ritualistic observance had the power to tear the early church apart. There really was a lot at stake here. If the Jewish converts had prevailed, Christianity would probably have become a minor Jewish sect with little reference to our central belief in salvation through grace, not ritual observance.

Genesis 25:21–28

Isaac prayed to the LORD on behalf of his wife, because she was childless. The LORD answered his prayer, and his wife Rebekah became pregnant. The babies jostled each other within her, and she said, 'Why is this happening to me?' So she went to inquire of the LORD. The LORD said to her,

'Two nations are in your womb, and two peoples from within you will be separated; one people will be stronger than the other, and the older will serve the younger.'

When the time came for her to give birth, there were twin boys in her womb. The first to come out was red, and his whole body was like a hairy garment; so they named him Esau. After this, his brother came out, with his hand grasping Esau's heel; so he was named Jacob. Isaac was sixty years old when Rebekah gave birth to them.

The boys grew up, and Esau became a skilful hunter, a man of the open country, while Jacob was content to stay at home among the tents. Isaac, who had a taste for wild game, loved Esau, but Rebekah loved Jacob.

Family therapists will be groaning at this point. In a few short verses we have a toxic mix: a prior struggle with infertility (in a culture that reveres childbearing), a pregnancy fraught with anxiety, topped off with a weird religious prophecy that counters the culture of the importance of the eldest son. The twins turn out to be different in almost every way with alpha-male Esau constantly upstaged by his cleverer younger brother, who also turns out to be the blatant favourite of his mother. This really is one of the epic feuds of the Old Testament and has the capacity to rival the Dassler brothers.

The theory

One tool we can use to help us understand conflict is an illustration known as the Conflict Curve, reproduced here. The idea has been around a long time but was probably promoted most strikingly by American writer Michael Lund, who used it in analysing international wars.[2] The key insight is that all conflicts go through a predictable pattern. Grasping this will help us to understand the bigger picture of what is happening, and also gives us the tools to address it most effectively. In making sense of this, note that the curve illustrates intensity of conflict on the vertical axis and time on the horizontal.

Conflict escalation and de-escalation curve

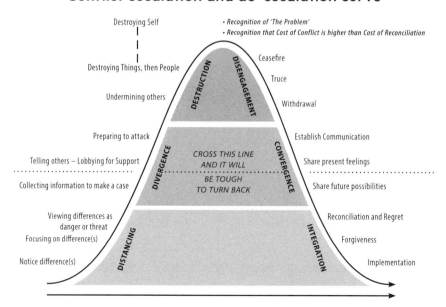

Stage one (distancing) is the 'latent conflict'. The conflict is simmering but has not yet erupted – perhaps due to politeness or the need to keep up appearances – so at this stage the conflict is still largely hidden. Eventually the tension can no longer be kept under wraps and intensifies (divergence) – as the curve angles up, there is a rapid increase in conflict level over a short period of time. Typically, this involves both sides recruiting to their cause, criticism of the 'opposition', and verbal and even physical aggression. At the top of the curve (destruction), we have open hostility. This is often extremely damaging in every sense, all-consuming and emotionally draining. At some point, either because of intervention or just because of exhaustion, the conflict starts to abate (disengagement); de-escalation takes place and there is some sort of negotiated future sketched out (convergence).

Now, because we 'don't do conflict', Christians are often in denial about what is happening, in normal secular environments but particularly in Christian ministry contexts. (You may later like to look at the Afterword as different personalities react differently to the stress of conflict and other tools such as Myers-Briggs or a DISC personality inventory may give us valuable insight.) Very often leaders tend to 'play down' any conflict with an assumption that we can sort it out. In my experience, we are nearly always much further up the curve than we want to admit, which is why conflicts can sometimes seem to erupt from nowhere, despite the reality that they have been brewing for a long time. Managing conflict is enormously complex. Are the people in conflict fearful of change or fearful of loss? I stress again, not all conflict is bad; fighting injustice involves conflict but the prize may be worth the pain (hence Jesus' comments in Luke 12:51).

Secondly, remember that the curve is not prescriptive – in other words, if we recognise what is going on at any point on the curve, we can cross to the other side and avoid the most destructive part of full conflict. Following the curve is *not* inevitable and early intervention is hugely important. Leaders take note: stop 'not dealing' with that conflict you have noticed. Dealing with it now may be difficult or embarrassing, but what the conflict curve tells us is that this will be easier than dealing with it later.

Thirdly, for many reasons, it may be better to work through the conflict curve to get to the other side. I grew up during the Cold War with the famous dictum of 'mutually assured destruction'. The prospect of mutual nuclear annihilation was a sort of peace, but frankly a dangerous, unstable and uncertain one. In our understanding we need to clarify the difference between being a peacekeeper (passive) and being a peacemaker (active). Jesus says, 'Blessed are the peacemakers', not, 'Blessed are the peacekeepers'. These words are so often confused or used interchangeably among Christians when they mean very different things. Are we peace *keepers* (in that sense), or peace *makers* (in the best possible sense)?

Fourthly, peacemaking is a serious and skilled business – if in doubt, get help. It can be a painful process that is time consuming and requires both sides to be able to express what has happened and why they have been hurt. Not for nothing was the Truth and Reconciliation Commission named that way in post-apartheid South Africa, a practical illustration of the need for truth (however painful) to be known before peace could be negotiated.[3] Because of our discomfort, Christians are prone to rushing this to get to the bottom of the curve. Many a well-meaning minister has invited the warring parties for a friendly cup of tea, only to be shocked at the expression of physical and verbal violence that follows. Get help.

Lastly, note that the 'post-conflict peacebuilding' can take many forms. Yes, there are wonderful stories of former enemies living together in peace and harmony... but, sometimes, a well-managed 'split' might be the best possible option. Be open to miracles but be realistic in the moment.

Back to scripture

Acts 15:5–14,19–21,24

Then some of the believers who belonged to the party of the Pharisees stood up and said, 'The Gentiles must be circumcised and required to keep the law of Moses.'

The apostles and elders met to consider this question. After much discussion, Peter got up and addressed them: 'Brothers, you know that some time ago God made a choice among you that the Gentiles might hear from my lips the message of the gospel and believe. God, who knows the heart, showed that he accepted them by giving the Holy Spirit to them, just as he did to us. He did not discriminate between us and them, for he purified their hearts by faith. Now then, why do you try to test God by putting on the necks of Gentiles a yoke that neither we nor our ancestors have been able to bear? No! We believe it is through the grace of our Lord Jesus that we are saved, just as they are.'

The whole assembly became silent as they listened to Barnabas and Paul telling about the signs and wonders God had done among the Gentiles through them. When they finished, James spoke up. 'Brothers,' he said, 'listen to me. Simon has described to us how God first intervened to choose a people for his name from the Gentiles. [...] It is my judgment, therefore, that we should not make it difficult for the Gentiles who are turning to God. Instead we should write to them, telling them to abstain from food polluted by idols, from sexual immorality, from the meat of strangled animals and from blood. For the law of Moses has been preached in every city from the earliest times and is read in the synagogues on every Sabbath.' [...] We have heard that some went out from us without our authorisation and disturbed you, troubling your minds by what they said.

In verse 1, Luke notes that the Jewish converts went straight into 'teaching the brothers'; there is no negotiation with the early church leadership. They are aware of the differences in approach, making a case and lobbying for support of their point of view. Paul and Barnabas arrive in Jerusalem to find that there is indeed a genuine conflict going on. The language of the party of the Pharisees is blunt, confrontational, and uncompromising. Paul and Barnabas together play the role of peacemaker and, crucially, manage to get both sides to talk (placing them about halfway up the conflict curve). Both sides are listened to and are able to express their view. In verse 7 we read the phrase, 'after much discussion' – getting *across* the conflict curve and starting to go down the other side takes immense amounts of time. Both sides need to feel that they have been heard – it is powerfully therapeutic to know your view has been genuinely understood, even if the final decision does not go your way. Active listening is a skill in itself and the basis of all the talking therapies, which is why practitioners are required to practise it so much. A simple example is to get each side to express their point of view, and then get the other side to try and reflect that back, taking turns to express the perspective that is not their own.

Note the final part of this passage: Christians tend to want to rush the second half of the curve. Part of the reconciliation and peacemaking process is to acknowledge the hurt that has been caused.

It's interesting that the eventual decision in this case is not a messy compromise (one side clearly 'wins'), yet the process has been restorative, and the immediate conflict is ended.

Returning now to our passage from Genesis, we read in chapter 27 of how the impulsive Esau 'sells' his birthright to the cunning Jacob, although the working out of this requires further deceit, as Jacob clearly recruits Rebekah to his cause. This ramps up the conflict to the almost-top level, with Esau threatening to destroy Jacob in Genesis 27:41. We come back to the story now in chapter 33.

Genesis 33:1–16

Jacob looked up and there was Esau, coming with his four hundred men; so he divided the children among Leah, Rachel and the two female servants. He put the female servants and their children in front, Leah and her children next, and Rachel and Joseph in the rear. He himself went on ahead and bowed down to the ground seven times as he approached his brother.

But Esau ran to meet Jacob and embraced him; he threw his arms around his neck and kissed him. And they wept. Then Esau looked up and saw the women and children. 'Who are these with you?' he asked.

Jacob answered, 'They are the children God has graciously given your servant.'

Then the female servants and their children approached and bowed down. Next, Leah and her children came and bowed down. Last of all came Joseph and Rachel, and they too bowed down.

Esau asked, 'What's the meaning of all these flocks and herds I met?'

'To find favour in your eyes, my lord,' he said.

But Esau said, 'I already have plenty, my brother. Keep what you have for yourself.'

'No, please!' said Jacob. 'If I have found favour in your eyes, accept this gift from me. For to see your face is like seeing the face of God, now that you have received me favourably. Please accept the present that was brought to you, for God has been gracious to me and I have all I need.' And because Jacob insisted, Esau accepted it.

Then Esau said, 'Let us be on our way; I'll accompany you.'

But Jacob said to him, 'My lord knows that the children are tender and that I must care for the ewes and cows that are nursing their young. If they are driven hard just one day, all the animals will die. So let my lord go on ahead of his servant, while I move along slowly at the pace of the flocks and herds before me and the pace of the children, until I come to my lord in Seir.'

Esau said, 'Then let me leave some of my men with you.'

'But why do that?' Jacob asked. 'Just let me find favour in the eyes of my lord.'

So that day Esau started on his way back to Seir. Jacob, however, went to Sukkoth, where he built a place for himself and made shelters for his livestock. That is why the place is called Sukkoth.

This meeting of Jacob and Esau is, I think, one of the most astonishing encounters of the Old Testament. Esau (the wronged brother) offers a truce – the first step to descending the conflict curve. Jacob's relief (in verse 10) is palpable. Deep communication takes place.

Time, literally years in this case, and geographic separation bring a measure of healing and the brothers are reconciled in Genesis 32–33. That both brothers are older, wiser, and wealthy seems to have taken the edge off their differences. Despite all this, it is not a simple happy ending. Perhaps wisely, Jacob chooses to maintain a geographic distance from Esau – clearly a carefully managed settlement!

And finally…

Some time ago, I was contacted by the head teacher of a large secondary school to see if I would broker a reconciliation discussion between two warring members of her science department. The conflict had classic ingredients of a slightly older and well experienced (male) teacher being overlooked for promotion in favour of an energetic and younger (female) teacher brought in from another school. Mandated to bring change and progress, each initiative of hers was construed by the older teacher as critical and antagonistic. Every comment of his was construed by the new younger leader as negative and resistant.

I mentioned that I was not a trained mediator but as I had met the head and she knew and trusted me, she still wanted me to do the work. After some consideration I printed off several copies of the conflict curve on A4 sheets of paper. With myself, the departmental head, a secretary to take notes, the two protagonists and their union representatives, there were seven of us sitting round a large table. I set some ground rules for listening, time limits and we then started a bruising two-hour discussion of the issues.

Eventually we came up with a plan for the two to meet on a regular basis to discuss issues before they could build into resentment (implicitly a recognition of the wisdom of action early on in the curve). In the best traditions of coaching, this plan came from them, not me, but what really intrigued me was that during the two hours, every single member of the meeting at some point picked up a copy of the conflict curve and used it to articulate or explain a point they were making. It was the perfect illustration of the power of tools to enable us to navigate what would otherwise just be abstract ideas and words.

CHAPTER 3: TIME MANAGEMENT

Or, what to do... now!

> *Carpe diem quam minimum credula postero.*
> *('Seize the day, trusting not the next one.')*
>
> **Horace**

This is my all-time favourite approach when I start getting into conversations about 'time management' – usually a euphemism for 'I'm struggling to organise my work and get it done' or, more prosaically, 'Help! I'm drowning.'

In 1967, Charles Hummel observed: 'The important task rarely must be done today, or even this week... But the urgent task calls for instant action... The momentary appeal of these tasks seems irresistible and important, and they devour our energy. But in the light of time's perspective, their deceptive prominence fades; with a sense of loss, we recall the vital tasks we pushed aside. We realize we've become slaves to the tyranny of the urgent.'[1] Interestingly, Hummel was a top-level US academic but also president of the US Intervarsity Christian Fellowship, so had a distinctly biblical approach. He uses the word 'vital' rather than 'important', but the root of this thinking tool is apparent.

I would suggest that Stephen Covey is the most prominent recent thinker in developing work in this area, and again recommend his book, *The 7 Habits of Highly Effective People*. This *carpe diem* time management tool is all about getting a grip on the to-do list that never seems to get any shorter.

Bible stories

Mark 1:32–37

That evening after sunset the people brought to Jesus all the sick and demon possessed. The whole town gathered at the door, and Jesus healed many who had various diseases. He also drove out many demons, but he would not let the demons speak because they knew who he was.

Very early in the morning, while it was still dark, Jesus got up, left the house, and went off to a solitary place, where he prayed. Simon and his companions went to look for him, and when they found him, they exclaimed: 'Everyone is looking for you!'

Omitting a birth narrative in his Gospel, Mark plunges straight into writing about Jesus' adult ministry. The pace of the story is breathtaking. Even before the end of chapter 1, we have multiple accounts of healing. The day is full and the evening no less hectic. Jesus rises before dawn to spend time in solitary devotion to His heavenly father, yet... His disciples search for Him and declare, 'Everyone is looking for you!'

This passage exquisitely encapsulates Jesus' divinity and humanity. The healings are a powerful demonstration of the power of God at work in His son yet, for this place and time, Jesus is restricted like any human. He can only be in one location and has the same length day as everyone. Time management and priorities are still real issues for Him to consider.

Luke 8:40–48

Now when Jesus returned, a crowd welcomed him, for they were all expecting him. Then a man named Jairus, a synagogue leader, came and fell at Jesus' feet, pleading with him to come to his house because his only daughter, a girl of about twelve, was dying.

As Jesus was on his way, the crowds almost crushed him. And a woman was there who had been subject to bleeding for twelve years, but no one could heal her. She came up behind him and touched the edge of his cloak, and immediately her bleeding stopped.

'Who touched me?' Jesus asked.

When they all denied it, Peter said, 'Master, the people are crowding and pressing against you.'

But Jesus said, 'Someone touched me; I know that power has gone out from me.'

Then the woman, seeing that she could not go unnoticed, came trembling and fell at his feet. In the presence of all the people, she told why she had touched him and how she had been instantly healed. Then he said to her, 'Daughter, your faith has healed you. Go in peace.'

The real-time sequencing of events here is beautifully captured by Luke. Jairus arrives to plead for his daughter. As compassionate humans, we sense the relief that he must feel, the hope that maybe this man, Jesus, can do something? Then the woman interferes. As is often the case, Luke's narrative is sparse in detail, yet we can imagine the whole entourage suddenly stopping as Jesus looks around and asks, 'Who touched me?' We sense the crowd's incomprehension – surely, He needs to get to the girl *now*, she is *dying*. What is Jesus going to do?

John 7:1–5

After this, Jesus went around in Galilee. He did not want to go about in Judea because the Jewish leaders there were looking for a way to kill him. But when the Jewish Festival of Tabernacles was near, Jesus' brothers said to him, 'Leave Galilee and go to Judea, so that your disciples there may see the works you do. No one who wants to become a public figure acts in secret. Since you are doing these things, show yourself to the world.' For even his own brothers did not believe in him.

This passage puts a fascinating twist on our thinking. This time it is not Jesus but His brothers who sense the urgency, trying to persuade Him to seize the moment and boost His own public profile. Again, Jesus can only be in one place and time and the sense of Him considering priorities and alternatives is very real.

The theory

Covey's insight is that everything on our 'to do' list can be put into one of four categories (see the diagram below). First, we have tasks that are urgent *and* important. Anyone working in an accident and emergency department will pretty much only ever deal with these types of tasks, though of course that is a specialised example. Whatever our workload, we'll know what our most pressing demands are. Typical examples we might encounter in Christian ministry may include pastoral emergencies, or a last-minute glitch like your speaker not turning up!

The second quadrant lists task that are important but not particularly urgent. Typically these might include: programme or budget planning; scheduled meetings; interviewing potential staff for a future appointment; planned pieces of work and study. Examples in education might include timetable planning or marking and reports that are not near their deadline. These things definitely matter, but aren't immediately time-sensitive.

The third quadrant contains non-important but urgent tasks. To begin with it might be hard to think of examples, but consider how often you have answered the phone only to be drawn into a long conversation you never intended to begin. The phone is, by definition, urgent. It will stop ringing if you don't answer it, but if you do, it frequently leads to work you may not really have time for. Often these are simple workplace distractions, or tasks you hope will take 'just a minute'...

The fourth quadrant contains tasks that are neither urgent nor important. Struggling to think of these? Covey lists 'sport' (though I personally disagree with this being unimportant!), but much more likely are those unscheduled minutes you wasted on social media.

The Important/Urgent matrix

	URGENT	NOT URGENT
IMPORTANT	Q1. Importand And Urgent	Q2. Important But Not Urgent
NOT IMPORTANT	Q3. Urgent But Not Important	Q4. Not Important And Not Urgent

A great way to get to grips with this and apply it to your own work is to create your own copy of the matrix (fairly simple to draw yourself, or print a blank template from the internet). Write on it what you have done over the last few days – not just the things in your diary but what you *actually did* in response to phone calls, emails etc.

Now, here is the crucial insight. Our work tends to be dominated by quadrant one – the urgent *and* important. But the box we really need to focus on is quadrant two – what is important but *not yet* urgent. Covey's genius observation is that when we don't address issues in box two, they will eventually migrate across into box one (lots of things become urgent if we wait long enough) and then we are back to a 'firefighting' style of work. We must do what is important, but most of us do it much better when we can approach this in a calm, considered manner. There will of course always be work that is important *and* urgent, but they key is to minimise the 'urgent' section.

We also need to try to be disciplined in eliminating work which is not important at all.

It is worth noting here that different personality types will find this relatively easy or difficult. I noticed when teaching at a theological college that some students loved to work right up to essay deadlines

– they needed the pressure (and consequent hit of adrenaline!) of the deadline to motivate them. If you are like this, you will have to work particularly hard at focusing on quadrant two tasks and incidentally, if you are in leadership, this style of working (always driven by approaching deadlines) may be particularly stressful for your team, even if you find it personally motivating. It may take considerable effort to transition from being driven by the demands of quadrant one to enjoying a more stable work life in quadrant two.

I'll say this again because I think it's important: transitioning to a quadrant two work style may take sustained effort! Guard also against those who perceive you as not having much on simply because your work is well organised and calm.

Covey's model sets us all sorts of indirect challenges. Some of us love the challenge of working last-minute; some of us want to be needed and letting tasks fall into box one is a great way of feeding this desire. We are also often working in an unhealthy culture (both secular and Christian) that lauds workaholism and busyness. A crucial factor for us as Christians is to both find our security and image in Christ, but also to be like Jesus in having a spiritual ear open to what God is calling us to do ('I only do what I see the father doing' – John 5:19).

Back to scripture

Mark 1:38–39

Jesus replied, 'Let us go somewhere else – to the nearby villages – so I can preach there also. That is why I have come.' So he travelled throughout Galilee, preaching in their synagogues and driving out demons.

Jesus has a powerful sense of both the urgent and important dimension of His work. He has risen early to pray. That's time which could be spent healing or teaching, but He has a sense of what is important *now*. His response to the disciples is not dismissive: having spent time in prayer, Jesus is happy to be drawn away to more preaching (and presumably teaching and healing). He has a sense of the importance of what He has to do ('That is why I have come'), but also has His priorities in order.

Luke 8:49–56

While Jesus was still speaking, someone came from the house of Jairus, the synagogue leader. 'Your daughter is dead,' he said. 'Don't bother the teacher anymore.'

Hearing this, Jesus said to Jairus, 'Don't be afraid; just believe, and she will be healed.'

When he arrived at the house of Jairus, he did not let anyone go in with him except Peter, John and James, and the child's father and mother. Meanwhile, all the people were wailing and mourning for her. 'Stop wailing,' Jesus said. 'She is not dead but asleep.'

They laughed at him, knowing that she was dead. But he took her by the hand and said, 'My child, get up!' Her spirit returned, and at once she stood up. Then Jesus told them to give her something to eat. Her parents were astonished, but he ordered them not to tell anyone what had happened.

Everyone thinks Jesus has blown it. Surely He could see that saving the girl was more important, more urgent than dealing with this middle-aged woman? I sometimes love to speculate on what's happening in Jesus' head, and in the heads of His disciples. Does He know what's about to happen, or is He just in tune with the Spirit and going with the flow? Either way, His sense of priorities is vindicated. The girl is healed, the sense of urgency (or lack of it) turns out to be for the best and God gets the glory.

John 7:6–11

Therefore Jesus told them, 'My time is not yet here; for you any time will do. The world cannot hate you, but it hates me because I testify that its works are evil. You go to the festival. I am not going up to this festival, because my time has not yet fully come.' After he had said this, he stayed in Galilee.

However, after his brothers had left for the festival, he went also, not publicly, but in secret. Now at the festival the Jewish leaders were watching for Jesus and asking, 'Where is he?'

This passage appears to show us things from a very different angle, not least in the sense of a much broader time frame for events. The sense of urgency is not coming from Jesus but His family and friends. One of the distinctive features of John's Gospel is the sense of timing and destiny that Jesus has. Buffeted by the expectations of His followers, it would have been easy to let events and the expectations of others set the pace, yet it is Jesus who effectively says, 'This is not urgent, I will do things in my Father's timing!'

There is another aspect of all this that I'd like us to consider here. The urgent/important matrix is absolutely consistent with a modern Western mentality that sees time as a commodity, like money, which we only have a certain amount of. Like budgeting, this tool helps us plan how to 'spend' what we have and save what we can (by avoiding those two bottom quadrants!). The very phrase 'time management' plays into this way of thinking. This is culturally pervasive but needs to be challenged with a different perspective. Bible scholars will know that the Old Testament approach to time was not oriented to quantity but *purpose*.

Ecclesiastes 3:1–5

There is a time for everything,
and a season for every activity under the heavens:
a time to be born and a time to die,
a time to plant and a time to uproot,
a time to kill and a time to heal,
a time to tear down and a time to build,
a time to weep and a time to laugh,
a time to mourn and a time to dance,
a time to scatter stones and a time to gather them,
a time to embrace and a time to refrain from embracing...

This approach to priorities is also evident in Jesus' own sense of destiny and timing. Pushed forward (perhaps into premature popularity) at the wedding in Cana, He declares to Mary, 'My hour has not yet come'. Jesus' ministry (much like Himself) is always an astonishing mixture of the human and divine. In John 7:1, He deliberately avoids Judea because of the real danger to His life, yet by 8:20 He is openly teaching in the Temple area. John's interpretation is that God's timing will not be thwarted or distorted by human actions, and a recurring phrase John uses in his writing is 'his time had not yet come'.

Chapter 11 of John's Gospel is a sustained and challenging exploration of the conflict between a purposeful (Hebraic) and commoditised (modern, worldly) approach to time. Lazarus is mortally ill. Jesus' location is not completely clear – John notes in 10:40 that He was where John himself had been baptising in the Jordan, but the observation in 11:18 that Bethany was 'less than two miles' from Jerusalem hints that Jesus was close by. Either way, Martha claims in verse 21 that Jesus' presence would have resulted in a different outcome, a suggestion echoed by Mary in verse 32. There is a heavy implication hanging in both statements: *'Surely You could have got here quicker? Why the lack of urgency? It wasn't far to come?'* Throughout the encounter, though, Jesus has been keeping time to a different drumbeat. Even from verse 4, right at the start of John's account, He has had a sense of God's *purpose* being worked out. It's a totally different way of looking at time.

The urgent/important matrix is a highly useful tool, but as followers of Jesus, we need to keep open to when God may have a different purpose that transcends the logic of good time management, and the countless opportunities He may have for us to experience the supernatural. Utilising the matrix well requires us to occasionally challenge some powerful cultural assumptions. I remember a friend of mine saying this to me in a conversation about this: 'Sometimes you have to do the unimportant and non-urgent if it feeds your soul.' That sounds fine in principle, but invites the consideration that if it is something that 'feeds our soul', it is *important* even if it's *not urgent*. If our soul is in dire need of feeding, it may be both urgent and important! There has been a significant cultural shift in the last decade or so to at last acknowledge the importance of acknowledging, managing and safeguarding our mental health. Despite this, many of us will still have difficulty deciding just which 'box' to put certain activities in.

In the mid-1930s, an eight-year-old German girl called Adelaide Delong was struggling with her maths homework. Her parents knew that their neighbour was good at maths so, armed with the bribe of a small piece of fudge, she went next door to get the help she needed (and returned with a cookie in exchange for the fudge!). The next-door neighbour was Albert Einstein, and her parents were mortified when they discovered who he was. He was delighted to help, and I am fascinated by the idea of the greatest mathematician in the world thinking, *'Now* is the time to help my neighbour's child with her maths homework!'

And finally...

We have already hinted at some of the challenging aspects of this time management tool. While it undoubtedly works, some of us may secretly not want it to work. For all sorts of reasons, we like the idea and image of being busy and driven by 'quadrant one' issues. To make this work may well require some significant soul searching – indeed it may require counselling or coaching or at least conversations with a trusted and honest friend.

There is also the issue of how you may be perceived by others. A well-organised person who appears to be on top of their workload in a hectic work culture may be perceived to be somewhat under-employed, and then given more tasks to do. There is a highly prevalent office culture which says, 'If you are not overwhelmed, you are not busy enough.' Maintaining a good work ethic around quadrant two activities will often require some basic tools to maintain boundaries including (for example) separate 'work' and 'home' phones and out-of-office email messages.

Covey explored this need to be (or *appear* to be) busy, calling it 'urgency addiction'.[2] I was once a representative of my employer on a big national project exploring how faith could be more effectively expressed through social action. Most of the other representatives were CEOs or at least directors of their organisations. We would meet in London with regular coffee breaks. As soon as each break was announced, at least three quarters of the participants would rush out the room and start making frantic phone calls. I was once left in the room with just one other participant (actually a very successful magazine editor). We looked at each other rather bemused and then both said, 'Do you think we should go and phone someone?' It is easy to mock, and I am sure that many of the calls really were necessary, but the projected image was also clear: 'Look at me, I'm really busy and important, and vital to the running of my organisation!'

Maintaining a work style that is focused on quadrant two can be particularly challenging when others do not work in this way. I was once coaching a senior executive in education. In conversation she expressed her resentment of the way big tasks would arrive just as she was lining up for a well-earned holiday. After some dialogue and reflection, we both worked out what was happening. Her boss was likewise lining up for a holiday and would aim (to use the old expression) to 'clear her desk'. I suspect this was as much about clearing her mind and conscience, but the result would be a range of big tasks being delegated into my client's urgent/important box just as she was trying to relax. We spent some time working out a coping strategy which involved starting the run up to a holiday earlier. It also involved her proactively contacting her boss and others to say something like, 'Is there anything you need me to deal with, because I am tidying up before my holiday and won't be starting any big tasks after Wednesday?' The implication being that if you try and dump something on me at the end of the week... you have been warned: it will have to wait.

Some of this chapter first appeared in a magazine article which I finished about a week before the deadline. Just as I ticked it off my list, I was contacted by my church small group leader. 'Someone is ill – could you lead the Bible study tonight?' Being on top of quadrant two work frees up time for those unexpected events in quadrant one. I was delighted to accept the invitation.

MANAGE

CHAPTER 4:
MANAGING CHANGE

How to initiate and manage change

To improve is to change; to be perfect is to change often.

Winston Churchill[1]

How many Pentecostals does it take to change a lightbulb?

Ten... one to change the bulb, and nine to pray against the spirit of darkness.

Of course, what makes lightbulb jokes funny is the fact that they are not really about lightbulbs at all, but about revealing the stereotyped behaviour that we recognise in each other when it comes to change.

'What people resist is not change per se, but loss,' says leadership guru Ronald Heifetz.[2] Experience in any organisation shows that change may bring loss, gain, the threat of loss, the opportunity for growth, and probably a mixture of all these things. Leading and managing a process of change is a major task. Most professionals (whether in the corporate world, education, industry, or ministry) are required to not only look after a static situation, but also to anticipate threats and developments, and manage a reaction to them. In this and the next chapter we will unpack the process of change, how people tend to react to change, and how we can manage those reactions well.

Bible stories

Exodus 3:7–8,10–14,16

The LORD said, 'I have indeed seen the misery of my people in Egypt.
I have heard them crying out because of their slave drivers, and I am
concerned about their suffering. So I have come down to rescue them
from the hand of the Egyptians and to bring them up out of that land
into a good and spacious land, a land flowing with milk and honey –
the home of the Canaanites, Hittites, Amorites, Perizzites, Hivites and
Jebusites. [...] So now, go. I am sending you to Pharaoh to bring my
people the Israelites out of Egypt.'

But Moses said to God, 'Who am I that I should go to Pharaoh and
bring the Israelites out of Egypt?'

And God said, 'I will be with you. And this will be the sign to you that
it is I who have sent you: When you have brought the people out of
Egypt, you will worship God on this mountain.'

Moses said to God, 'Suppose I go to the Israelites and say to them,
'The God of your fathers has sent me to you,' and they ask me, "What is
his name?" Then what shall I tell them?'

God said to Moses, 'I AM WHO I AM. This is what you are to say to
the Israelites: "I am has sent me to you." [...] Go, assemble the elders of
Israel and say to them, "The LORD, the God of your fathers – the God of
Abraham, Isaac and Jacob – appeared to me and said: I have watched
over you and have seen what has been done to you in Egypt."'

The Exodus is a key step in God's mission to redeem humankind. It marks
the start of His establishing salvation through a chosen people group
(and ultimately through Jesus). Moreover, the way God chooses to rescue
reveals much about Himself. God works in partnership with His created
people. No odds, risk, oppression, or jeopardy is too hard for Him to
overcome. God requires His people to step out in faith and ultimately
to claim what is promised. This passage effectively marks Moses'
commissioning as leader, and we will explore the process of change as
this commissioning is worked out.

The theory

Our theory is the eight-step change model developed over 40 years by the highly respected John Kotter, a global management and leadership expert. Kotter's implicit observation is that change invariably causes some reaction. Almost no management processes happen in a vacuum. To do one thing challenges another option or unbalances the status quo. Change will always work against some form of resistance or inertia. Kotter's theory breaks this apparently confusing process into identifiable steps that map what is required to not just make change but sustain it in the long term. Here are the steps with just a brief explanation (if you research this theory more elsewhere, please note that different authors may use slightly different terminology):

1: Create urgency. This may be the hardest step. Most organisations have survived past threats and strains. To manage change, your role as leader is to convince those inside and outside of your organisation that major change is imperative for success or even survival.

2: Form a powerful coalition. As Christians, we love the lone prophetic voice. Historically we revere great leaders who 'saved' their organisation or country. The reality is that you are much more likely to succeed if you campaign successfully for change within your organisation. Talk the plan through with key stakeholders and get a groundswell of support (or at least openness) before a vital meeting.

3: Create a vision for change. Many of us are, frankly, unimaginative. This stage is not just about logic but about inspiration, and you need people to 'get it'. As Stephen Covey observes, 'All things are created twice; first mentally; then physically.'[3] The key to creativity is to begin with the end in mind, with a vision and a blueprint of the desired result.' In leading change, you may have a clear image of what the end product is, but it may take huge effort to communicate this effectively to your team or investors.

4: Communicate the vision. It is still embryonic and vulnerable. Talk about the vision; share; get excited; take people to see it working somewhere. This is a further progression of the previous step. At this stage people are open to the possibilities, but are not necessarily intellectually or emotionally committed. Be open to almost anything that will convince them it can happen.

5: Remove obstacles. An obstacle could be a practical issue that needs addressing, perhaps to do with logistics, staffing or space – or, as brutal as it sounds, it could be a person, who simply refuses to come onboard with the plan. This stage marks a definitive shift from inspiration to practical action.

6: Celebrate even the little wins. Change is particularly hard when there is little short-term benefit, in fact disruption and cost mean that change is frequently negative in the short term. It takes courage for an organisation to hold its nerve and look for long-term gains. Rejoice in anything that is a 'first fruit' benefit. It's OK to create opportunities for lots of little wins to be easily achieved if it's going to boost morale.

7: Build on the change. Reflect on what went well when you succeed, and consider how you could do it even better. This may be particularly significant if the change has resulted in new working practices. However successful, there may be a sense of unease and disquiet. New practices are not routine or comfortable. Some self-awareness of this is important. Verbally processing every aspect helps embed new ways of working.

8: Anchor the changes in culture. Make sure practices reflect the new ways of working and continue to do so until it is second nature. This last step is one of Kotter's strongest observations. Organisational culture is astonishingly powerful and even after all the time, effort and cost of change, organisations can slip back into their old way of trying to do things.

The real value of Kotter's model is that it gives us a 'road map' of change. It helps us to measure progress and, critically, not try to jump too far ahead. It is also a salutary warning regarding the range of skills needed for successful change (hence step 2). As leader, you may be the only one who has discovered this tool but, paradoxically, what Kotter teaches is the huge range of gifts you need to harness for successful change. Visionaries by definition tend to not understand why we can't just do it *now*! The end goal is obvious to them, but others may not share their enthusiasm. You need 'big picture' people with vision and charisma for the early stages, but you also need those who are spectacularly good at detail by the time you get to steps 5 and onwards. High levels of persuasive people skills are needed in the early stages, and discipline is needed later. Few people are good at all these so excellent levels of self-awareness are required for managers of change.

Kotter's model is, of course, not perfect. Like many theories, it was developed in a high-level corporate environment and may need some level of adapting to small, informal, or voluntary organisations. The model does not explicitly address an organisation's legacy or approach to culture. Has the organisation tried to change in the past and failed? Kotter's focus is on the challenge of organisational change and ignores the implications of personal change that inevitably accompany that. Many organisations (and indeed individuals) may feel this approach is cavalier and want a greater consideration of personal consequences of change. Furthermore, it does not explicitly acknowledge more modern or alternative methods of organisation (which we will consider in chapter 9) and assumes at least some level of 'top down' hierarchical management structure.

Despite all this, Kotter is still arguably the market leader in change planning, well tried and trusted.

Back to scripture

We are going to consider Kotter's model as we continue working through the Exodus narrative as Moses tries to bring massive change to almost every aspect of life.

Step 1: Create urgency

Exodus 5:10–11,14–17,20–21

Then the slave drivers and the overseers went out and said to the people, 'This is what Pharaoh says: "I will not give you any more straw. Go and get your own straw wherever you can find it, but your work will not be reduced at all."' [...] And Pharaoh's slave drivers beat the Israelite overseers they had appointed, demanding, 'Why haven't you met your quota of bricks yesterday or today, as before?'

Then the Israelite overseers went and appealed to Pharaoh: 'Why have you treated your servants this way? Your servants are given no straw, yet we are told, "Make bricks!" Your servants are being beaten, but the fault is with your own people.'

Pharaoh said, 'Lazy, that's what you are – lazy! That is why you keep saying, "Let us go and sacrifice to the LORD."' [...] When they left Pharaoh, they found Moses and Aaron waiting to meet them, and they said, 'May the LORD look on you and judge you! You have made us obnoxious to Pharaoh and his officials and have put a sword in their hand to kill us.'

In the tradition of all great dictators, Pharaoh's response to the appeal for even limited freedom is to ramp up the pressure and crush any aspirations the Israelites might have. A situation that has been difficult and intolerable is made unbearable and unsustainable. Notice also that despite the vison and promise of a better life, opposition is building (a theme we will come back to). Despite his best intentions, Moses has genuinely made the situation worse. Urgency is building.

Step 2: Form a powerful coalition

Exodus 3:16,18

'Go, assemble the elders of Israel and say to them, "The LORD, the God of your fathers – the God of Abraham, Isaac and Jacob – appeared to me and said: I have watched over you and have seen what has been done to you in Egypt.' [...] The elders of Israel will listen to you. Then you and the elders are to go to the king of Egypt and say to him, "The LORD, the God of the Hebrews, has met with us. Let us take a three-day journey into the wilderness to offer sacrifices to the LORD our God."'

Here we have the Lord speaking to Moses. The Old Testament elders (literally 'the bearded ones') would be heads of families and tribes. Respected for their age, wisdom and experience, their duties included judicial arbitration and military service. Why would they listen to a returning, disgraced, privileged leader?

The perceived need for leaders to be charismatic orators is not new. In Exodus 4:10, Moses complains that he 'has never been eloquent'; that he is 'slow of speech and tongue'. Famously God then sends Moses' brother Aaron to be the mouthpiece of the team. Again, notice this example of Kotter's emphasis on the need for different gifts (which come packaged in different people) in the process.

Leadership can be lonely. But the assurance from God remains to Moses: you will not be alone.

Step 3: Create a vision for change

Exodus 3:17

And I have promised to bring you up out of your misery in Egypt into the land of the Canaanites, Hittites, Amorites, Perizzites, Hivites and Jebusites – a land flowing with milk and honey.

Familiarity with this slogan blunts its impact. For an oppressed people – oppressed not just in slavery but in harsh, forced labour – the concept of owning any land would be a dream. A land that is fertile and productive seems even less possible. That such a land would already be occupied would be no surprise but that they might one day own it for themselves would be beyond their wildest imagination. Hope thrives on vision.

Step 4: Communicate the vision

Exodus 4:29 – 5:1

Moses and Aaron brought together all the elders of the Israelites, and Aaron told them everything the LORD had said to Moses. He also performed the signs before the people, and they believed. And when they heard that the LORD was concerned about them and had seen their misery, they bowed down and worshipped.

Afterward Moses and Aaron went to Pharaoh and said, 'This is what the LORD, the God of Israel, says: "Let my people go, so that they may hold a festival to me in the wilderness."'

Despite the omission of detail, Exodus still gives us an extraordinarily comprehensive account of the process. As instructed, Moses and Aaron start to communicate the vision to the people, but they also need to start negotiating with Pharaoh and the existing power structures. Vision is not just about abstract belief; it needs to be fleshed out with plans and targets. This may well explain the request for a three-day festival in the desert. It is a small part of God's bigger redemptive plan, but it is one the people can start to imagine – a cognitive stepping stone on a much longer journey.

Step 5: Remove obstacles

Exodus 7:14–16,20–24

Then the LORD said to Moses, 'Pharaoh's heart is unyielding; he refuses to let the people go. Go to Pharaoh in the morning as he goes out to the river. Confront him on the bank of the Nile, and take in your hand the staff that was changed into a snake. Then say to him, "The LORD, the God of the Hebrews, has sent me to say to you: let my people go, so that they may worship me in the wilderness. But until now you have not listened."' [...] Moses and Aaron did just as the LORD had commanded. He raised his staff in the presence of Pharaoh and his officials and struck the water of the Nile, and all the water was changed into blood. The fish in the Nile died, and the river smelled so bad that the Egyptians could not drink its water.

But the Egyptian magicians did the same things by their secret arts, and Pharaoh's heart became hard; he would not listen to Moses and Aaron, just as the LORD had said. Instead, he turned and went into his palace, and did not take even this to heart. And all the Egyptians dug along the Nile to get drinking water, because they could not drink the water of the river.

Opposition to change is highly predictable. To find ourselves 'pushing an open door' is a rare delight. In this passage, the vested interests in Egypt are well established and hugely powerful. The plagues are of course a systematic series of incidents to show the power of the God of the Israelites. They ascend in severity, ending with the harrowing death of the firstborns (Exodus 11). The impact of this is greater than we can perceive, it is not just a personal tragedy but deeply symbolic. Firstborn sons received a disproportionate share of the inheritance. To kill the firstborns was to effectively disrupt the whole future of family and nation. It would be deeply emblematic and destabilising to the Egyptian culture.

Step 6: Celebrate even the little wins

Exodus 14:21–28

Then Moses stretched out his hand over the sea, and all that night the LORD drove the sea back with a strong east wind and turned it into dry land. The waters were divided, and the Israelites went through the sea on dry ground, with a wall of water on their right and on their left.

The Egyptians pursued them, and all Pharaoh's horses and chariots and horsemen followed them into the sea. During the last watch of the night the Lord looked down from the pillar of fire and cloud at the Egyptian army and threw it into confusion. He jammed the wheels of their chariots so that they had difficulty driving. And the Egyptians said, 'Let's get away from the Israelites! The LORD is fighting for them against Egypt.'

Then the LORD said to Moses, 'Stretch out your hand over the sea so that the waters may flow back over the Egyptians and their chariots and horsemen.' Moses stretched out his hand over the sea, and at daybreak the sea went back to its place. The Egyptians were fleeing toward it, and the LORD swept them into the sea. The water flowed back and covered the chariots and horsemen – the entire army of Pharaoh that had followed the Israelites into the sea. Not one of them survived.

Despite the drama of the Passover and night-time escape, the Israelites are far from safe. The desire to return to captivity is a recurring complaint (see 14:11–12), and God shows a tender awareness of this in the plan (see 13:17, where He shows great concern for their wellbeing and the risk of war, and leads them through a safer route). Despite this apparent vulnerability in the plan, the Red Sea crossing is still a powerful early win. It is a dramatic marker of the transition from captivity to freedom. It is also again revealing of the character of God – a God who rescues (through water, foreshadowing baptism) and sustains those He calls. These are the first, faith-growing steps and examples of what is possible.

Step 7: Build on the change

Exodus 16:11–16,19–20

The LORD said to Moses, 'I have heard the grumbling of the Israelites. Tell them, "At twilight you will eat meat, and in the morning you will be filled with bread. Then you will know that I am the LORD your God."'

That evening quail came and covered the camp, and in the morning there was a layer of dew around the camp. When the dew was gone, thin flakes like frost on the ground appeared on the desert floor. When the Israelites saw it, they said to each other, 'What is it?' For they did not know what it was.

Moses said to them, 'It is the bread the LORD has given you to eat. This is what the LORD has commanded: "Everyone is to gather as much as they need. Take an omer for each person you have in your tent."' [...] Then Moses said to them, 'No one is to keep any of it until morning.'

However, some of them paid no attention to Moses; they kept part of it until morning, but it was full of maggots and began to smell. So Moses was angry with them.

Again, God is doing two things at once here. The ostensible and very immediate need is for food. God provides this, but with a fascinating coda to the story: it is about generosity and sustaining, but clearly it is also about teaching the Israelites to trust. Those who stockpile the gift find it rots. God does the practical but also reveals His character: a sustainer who can be trusted.

Step 8: Anchor the change in culture

Exodus 19:3–6

Then Moses went up to God, and the LORD called to him from the mountain and said, 'This is what you are to say to the descendants of Jacob and what you are to tell the people of Israel: "You yourselves have seen what I did to Egypt, and how I carried you on eagles' wings and brought you to myself. Now if you obey me fully and keep my covenant, then out of all nations you will be my treasured possession. Although the whole earth is mine, you will be for me a kingdom of priests and a holy nation." These are the words you are to speak to the Israelites.'

This story is the precursor to the delivery of the Ten Commandments, and ultimately the Old Testament law. It is profound in marking out God's nation from those around it – its different theology and practices. Geographical space from the oppression in Egypt has been a vital first step but this marks a further revelation of God's character.

Peter Drucker famously said, 'Culture eats strategy for breakfast.' My favourite definition of culture is, 'the way we do things round here'.[4] Culture is often even more powerful for not being written down. We all know what to expect, for example, if we go to a wedding, a book launch, or a business meeting. We don't generally need it explaining. Unless something very unusual is going to happen, we have a powerful set of cultural 'rules' that we tend to follow. These rules tend to be good at preserving things. They make us feel safe and comfortable (consider what happens in your own church) but can be massive barriers to embedding and maintaining change once it has happened. Kotter is right to emphasise the importance of this and many plans have faltered at this stage, not because the plan was flawed but because human insecurity and the powerful tendency to stick with 'the way we do things round here' crushes the new. Speaking metaphorically, the temptation to 'return to Egypt' can have a compelling attraction in the insecurity of the 'new'.

Kotter wrote several books, some of his later work focusing specifically on why change fails. In *Leading Change*,[5] he proposes eight reasons why change projects fail – perhaps not surprisingly reflecting strongly the eight steps of how they can work. If you are embarking on a major change project, I really recommend you do some more reading and research of your own.

And finally…

Several years ago, I took over leadership of a schools work charity based in an English city. It had a long history of good work (both pastoral and more overtly missional), but I sensed as I joined that the secondary section (the high school work with students aged 11 to 18) simply wasn't working. I had inherited the line management of two other staff members and a policy largely based on offering schools a range of RE lessons. The problem was mainly that the take-up of lessons seemed to be relentlessly dropping even though nothing about the lessons themselves had changed, and this had been a broadly successful strategy for engagement with the schools in the past.

In hindsight, step one (creating urgency for change) was relatively easy – it was possible to plot the take-up of lessons and the 'not working' feeling was clearly an accurate perception. However, even this stage had its difficulties. Opposition to the organisation tended to be interpreted through a particular spiritual paradigm – opposition was seen as spiritual warfare and was to be combatted with prayer and fasting rather than considering how we could offer a better 'product' to the schools.

I am not sure I ever formed a 'coalition', but certain key stakeholders did become very significant. I manged to interview a sympathetic deputy head who explained that RE itself was a declining subject in many schools. Most had minimised its place on the timetable, had few or no RE specialist staff and would often ditch RE lessons at crucial times of year to gain more time for exam revision. In practice, schools felt that they were largely judged on Maths, English and to a slightly lesser extent, the Sciences as key subjects. They knew that poor provision of RE simply would not affect them. In addition, the secular humanist culture of education had significantly developed. Where once we (at the schools' work charity) were seen to be offering something different that might give an alternative viewpoint and enrich young people's education, now we were viewed suspiciously as religious zealots who might try to indoctrinate their young people. Even to invite us in was a risk they did not need to take (remember step 2).

Further conversations with school staff revealed a new way of engaging that might open doors. What was clear was that schools were facing overwhelming pastoral needs in their young people, many of whom came from fairly dysfunctional households. From this we developed a vision for a chaplaincy style of working (inspired by what one bishop described as 'holy hanging around'), sending a qualified worker into school to spend time both one-to-one coaching specific young people, but also developing informal relationships in the best tradition of youth work (steps 3 and 4). The vision was created and communicated… but did then receive opposition (step 5).

Interestingly, most of this opposition was internal to the organisation, not from the schools (many of whom actually welcomed the plan). Some of the team felt it was too vague. They could get their heads around delivering a lesson but the idea of working within conversations that were less structured did not appeal. Interestingly, I also found opposition from my board of trustees, and I eventually traced this to the word 'chaplain'. Many had had negative experiences of chaplains either in the armed forces or other contexts. Chaplains were seen as failed ministers who had been side-lined into a safe and innocuous context where they could not do too much damage.

Launching the new work was tough (step 6). It became clear that the vision was not compatible with those staff members, so they transitioned into new roles while we brought on a qualified worker who could both 'get' the vision and do the work. Within 12 months of the new appointment, one of the major secondary schools asked us to do a week's 'mission', building on our new chaplaincy work. The school had a

Church of England ethos but had done little with it, and the mission was seen as a way of fulfilling this. Even so, there was a lot of nervousness as moved forward, and we were warned that if OFSTED turned up, the whole project would be ditched. In practice, it was a success (step 7), to the extent that the headteacher said that in future if OFSTED did arrive, she would emphasise the project and would frankly love them to see it.

We later followed up with a significantly sized 'enquirers group' for young people wishing to explore faith more, embedding faith exploration into the culture of the school and ensuring it had not been just a one off (step 8).

As with all tools, Kotter's plan is here to serve us, not the other way round. Real life is messy. This approach is a checklist and map, not a straitjacket. Absorb its wisdom but adapt it intelligently for your context.

CHAPTER 5: ADOPTING CHANGE

There is nothing more difficult to take in hand, more perilous to conduct, or more uncertain in its success, than to take the lead in the introduction of a new order of things.

Niccolo Machiavelli, *The Prince*

Managing change in your organisation or ministry can be a major task. Whilst Kotter looks at how change is led within your organisation, the tool we'll explore in this chapter is not about you but the people you work for (perhaps your team, or maybe even your customers). How are they likely to react? Will they welcome the change as it addresses long-standing problems and inefficiencies, or will they resent it as proof that 'constant change is here to stay'? Despite a self-evident need for improvement, many of us have a natural reluctance to alter the status quo despite Bono's observation that 'Saying no to change is a sad kind of stasis.'[1] Insight and understanding here are vital in helping us to hold on to the vision and explain why people might (or might not) welcome what is happening.

Bible stories

We are going to focus on two main passages but also explore this through other scriptures later.

First up: Nicodemus. There is a lovely little biblical detective story here! We meet Nicodemus (as does Jesus) by night in John 3. He is cautious but still curious:

John 3:1–12

Now there was a Pharisee, a man named Nicodemus who was a member of the Jewish ruling council. He came to Jesus at night and said, 'Rabbi, we know that you are a teacher who has come from God. For no one could perform the signs you are doing if God were not with him.'

Jesus replied, 'Very truly I tell you, no one can see the kingdom of God unless they are born again.'

'How can someone be born when they are old?' Nicodemus asked. 'Surely they cannot enter a second time into their mother's womb to be born!'

Jesus answered, 'Very truly I tell you, no one can enter the kingdom of God unless they are born of water and the Spirit. Flesh gives birth to flesh, but the Spirit gives birth to spirit. You should not be surprised at my saying, "You must be born again." The wind blows wherever it pleases. You hear its sound, but you cannot tell where it comes from or where it is going. So it is with everyone born of the Spirit.'

'How can this be?' Nicodemus asked.

'You are Israel's teacher,' said Jesus, 'and do you not understand these things? Very truly I tell you, we speak of what we know, and we testify to what we have seen, but still you people do not accept our testimony. I have spoken to you of earthly things and you do not believe; how then will you believe if I speak of heavenly things?'

Nicodemus has every reason to resist the change and threat of the 'Kingdom' that Jesus preaches. To say he is invested in the status quo is a massive understatement. He is a teacher, a rabbi, a priest. His status, identity and income are all tied up in a traditional understanding of the Jewish religion yet somewhere deep inside, his intellectual honesty demands that he investigate Jesus' teaching. He recognises something of the validity of Jesus' ministry that challenges his natural reluctance.

Next up: Paul and Agrippa. Paul is supposed to be defending himself in court in Caesarea but uses the opportunity to preach the gospel to Festus and Agrippa.

Acts 26:1–8,22–27

Then Agrippa said to Paul, 'You have permission to speak for yourself.'

So Paul motioned with his hand and began his defence: 'King Agrippa, I consider myself fortunate to stand before you today as I make my defence against all the accusations of the Jews, and especially so because you are well acquainted with all the Jewish customs and controversies. Therefore, I beg you to listen to me patiently. The Jewish people all know the way I have lived ever since I was a child, from the beginning of my life in my own country, and also in Jerusalem. They have known me for a long time and can testify, if they are willing, that I conformed to the strictest sect of our religion, living as a Pharisee. And now it is because of my hope in what God has promised our ancestors that I am on trial today. This is the promise our twelve tribes are hoping to see fulfilled as they earnestly serve God day and night. King Agrippa, it is because of this hope that these Jews are accusing me. Why should any of you consider it incredible that God raises the dead? [...] But God has helped me to this very day; so I stand here and testify to small and great alike. I am saying nothing beyond what the prophets and Moses said would happen – that the Messiah would suffer and, as the first to rise from the dead, would bring the message of light to his own people and to the Gentiles.'

At this point Festus interrupted Paul's defence. 'You are out of your mind, Paul!' he shouted. 'Your great learning is driving you insane.'

'I am not insane, most excellent Festus,' Paul replied. 'What I am saying is true and reasonable. The king is familiar with these things, and I can speak freely to him. I am convinced that none of this has escaped his notice, because it was not done in a corner. King Agrippa, do you believe the prophets? I know you do.'

It is easy to miss the drama here. Paul's liberty (and possibly his life) is at stake. This is not just intellectual sparring: a lot will depend on the outcome.

The theory

We have Everett Rogers to thank for a set of ideas which has been around since 1962. Rogers' theory of 'Diffusion of Innovation' (to give it the correct title) looks at how an idea gains momentum, gets traction and spreads through a group or society. In our context, the 'idea' might be your new way of working, a technological innovation, doing a new type of youth work or ministry – or it might be the gospel itself.

Rogers' insight here is to observe that all of us will fall into one of five 'adopter categories' in terms of our reaction to innovation and change. Roger's proposes a traditional bell curve distribution of possibilities (see diagram):

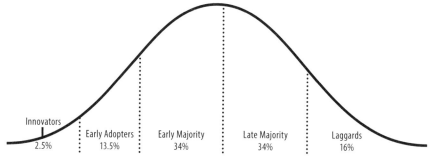

The five adopter categories Rogers proposes are:

- **Innovators** (2.5% of the people): Often leaders themselves, they can tolerate risk and are highly focused on trying new things.

- **Early adopters** (13.5%): Again, many of these will be leaders, aware of the need for change and tolerant of the cost of change.

- **Early majority** (34%): These like to see the evidence for the benefit of change but are still willing and happy to change before most. Strategies and logical reasons for the innovation appeal to them.

- **Late majority** (34%): Sceptical of change, these prefer to adopt it only after others have tried it. Evidential proof of success is a powerful motivator to this group.

- **Laggards** (16%): These people are very conservative, traditional and highly doubtful. Strategies to get them on board include personal appeal from the other groups and indeed, fear of what will happen if change is thwarted.

As always, it is worth noting that there is no 'correct' position to adopt – indeed you may find yourself in different categories on different issues. Most of us can think of great innovations the Church could have adopted faster/sooner (such as running Alpha courses; Messy Church; using social media etc) but can also think of a few non-starters we pursued where it really might have been better if the laggards had won!

As with all great theories, many other thinkers have built on Rogers' work. In 1991, Geoffrey Moore proposed that the boundary between 'early adopters' and the 'early majority' represented the crucial tipping point beyond which an idea was likely to gain critical mass (the minimum uptake to sustain acceptance), and widespread adoption. It is generally accepted now that once adoption reaches the early majority, it will not stop. Adoption in itself becomes an inexorable force with its own momentum and needing relatively little proactive promotion. (Many of us will know the feeling of seeing a new development coming at work. We haven't adopted it yet, but it is clear which way things are going.)

One of the strengths of Rogers' theory is that it gives us some solid indicators around what factors will help or hinder the diffusion and adoption of new practices. First are factors around the innovation itself. Is it radical, difficult, expensive, or simply a more substantial development of something that already exists?

Pioneer adopters are crucial, hence our current fascination with 'influencers'. Even in the 1960s, Rogers drew on the work of Lazarsfeld and Katz to talk about 'opinion leadership' within social networks.[2] All ideas and innovations need 'champions' who promote them – specifically champions who don't have a vested interest in the success of the change. There is a substantial challenge to us here as leaders and managers: what do we do if we are a natural 'laggard'? Innovations stretch teams and it can be highly stressful to be invited to lead a team into a process of change that we do not personally believe in.

Rogers also noted the importance of 'heterophily' and 'homophily'. Put simply, we tend to hang around with people like us. Diffusion may spread very rapidly within certain groups or classes but can be very resistant to crossing over into different groups.

It is also worth distinguishing between 'adoption' and 'diffusion'. The latter is the spread of the idea or practice across an identifiable society or group, whereas the former is an individual process. Rogers broke this down into five stages:

1. Knowledge/awareness: This is the individual's first encounter but at this stage they have little information and no commitment to the new idea.

2. Persuasion: The individual is now actively interested and seeking information.

3. Decision: This is a highly individualistic step, drawing on the core evaluation and decision-making process of the individual.

4. Implementation: The individual uses the new way of doing things and initially evaluates its effectiveness. Action has happened but commitment may still not be complete.

5. Confirmation/continuation: The individual embeds the new process in both thinking and practice. They continue to use it but may also be seeking cognitive affirmation that they have made the right decision.

Back to scripture

First, let's return to Nicodemus. I mentioned that there was a biblical detective story here...

We do not have a precise chronology of John's Gospel, but by chapter 7 we are probably well into Jesus' third year of ministry, and opposition is building from the established religious leaders. Despite this, Nicodemus' restraint clearly shows that he was wavering intellectually regarding the validity of Jesus' claim to messiahship:

John 7:50–52

Nicodemus, who had gone to Jesus earlier and who was one of their own number, asked, 'Does our law condemn a man without first hearing him to find out what he has been doing?'

They replied, 'Are you from Galilee, too? Look into it, and you will find that a prophet does not come out of Galilee.'

John 19:38–39

Later, Joseph of Arimathea asked Pilate for the body of Jesus. Now Joseph was a disciple of Jesus, but secretly because he feared the Jewish leaders. With Pilate's permission, he came and took the body away. He was accompanied by Nicodemus, the man who earlier had visited Jesus at night. Nicodemus brought a mixture of myrrh and aloes, about seventy-five pounds.

By John 19, after the crucifixion of Jesus, Nicodemus seems to be finally out in the open in his support of Christ's claims. It's hard to hide the fact that you are carrying 30 kilograms of spices to a tomb in broad daylight. Nicodemus is a classic 'laggard': he takes an age to 'get it'; is fearful and conservative; a pillar of the threatened establishment... but eventually he makes the intellectual jump.

Just to demonstrate how these judgments are subjective, I am portraying Nicodemus as a laggard. Compared to most of the Jewish hierarchy, however, he might be considered an early adopter!

Next, we rejoin Paul and Agrippa in Acts 26. This account has a less happy ending, despite Paul's oratorical skill and almost manipulative use of the context. Agrippa controlled the temple treasury and had power to appoint the high priest. He would be consulted by the Romans on religious matters because of his local knowledge and consequently could not afford to be seen to be publicly dismissive of Paul's claims: 'Then

Agrippa said to Paul, "Do you think that in such a short time you can persuade me to be a Christian?"' (v28).

This verse is almost comic. It is as if Agrippa is saying, 'I'm not an early adopter, you know!'

Paul replies, 'Short time or long, I pray [that] you may become what I am,' – a nice acknowledgement that it sometimes doesn't matter how long it takes. Be a laggard if you want, but just get there.

I'd like to consider a couple more biblical examples keeping Rogers' theory in mind. Many of us will be familiar with the miraculous results of the Day of Pentecost: 'Those who accepted his message were baptised, and about three thousand were added to their number that day' (Acts 2:41). But notice what also happens in the following days as described in verse 47: '... praising God and enjoying the favour of all the people. And the Lord added to their number daily those who were being saved.'

Rogers notes that the degree of compatibility of the new idea with the old is likely to push more people into early adoption. On the day of Pentecost, Peter preaches to Jews – they are already looking for the Messiah, and they understand the idea of atonement and that blood is spilt for sins. It is a much smaller intellectual step for them to adopt the new idea than in the many later situations where Paul preaches to Gentiles who have none of these presuppositions. Even with that advantage, the chapter ends with the Lord adding 'daily to their number'. Even with the best evangelistic talk, some people still need to take their time and think things through.

Matthew 13:3–9

Then he told them many things in parables, saying: 'A farmer went out to sow his seed. As he was scattering the seed, some fell along the path, and the birds came and ate it up. Some fell on rocky places, where it did not have much soil. It sprang up quickly, because the soil was shallow. But when the sun came up, the plants were scorched, and they withered because they had no root. Other seed fell among thorns, which grew up and choked the plants. Still other seed fell on good soil, where it produced a crop – a hundred, sixty or thirty times what was sown.

Whoever has ears, let them hear.'

I love how this parable Jesus tells provides both an illustration of Rogers' theory, but also a critique of it. The 'shallow soil' hearers are early adopters – open to change but perhaps lacking the imagination to see some of the implications. Those who are by character and nature 'early adopters' may well have moved on to something else by the time the 'majority' get there! By definition, the 'good' or 'deep' soil takes time – the late adopters may be slow but have counted the long-term cost and have a (literally) deeper commitment.

And finally...

The story of the Swiss watchmaking industry is now the stuff of business legend. The Swiss had been pre-eminent makers of watches and timepieces for decades. Despite this, the seeds of decline had been sowed in the invention of quartz technology in the early twentieth century. Scientists had discovered that applying an electric current across a quartz crystal caused it to vibrate with an astonishing degree of accuracy. Initially the practicality of this was limited by other aspects of electronic technology (such as the size of valves, and the non-existence of transistors) and the technology was confined to the world of university research clocks, being both rare and expensive.

The explosion of transistor technology in the late 1960s caused all this to change, and suddenly quartz technology made cheap, small wristwatches possible. It is business myth that the Swiss did not have this technology. They did, but what is clear is that they were slow to adopt it – indeed it was resisted through the retail chain. Quartz watches were cheap to produce, which meant less profit for manufacturers, importers, and retailers. Swiss makers tried to trade on their prestige and history, which meant that in the early 1980s, a five-dollar Mickey Mouse watch from Disneyland was technically more accurate than a two-thousand-dollar Rolex. Swiss manufacturers did eventually adopt quartz technology on a wide scale, but by then their watch making lead had been lost to Japanese brands like Casio and Seiko. The Japanese had been 'early adopters' and made a fortune, whereas the Swiss had been 'laggards' and paid a heavy price for it. By the mid-1980s, Swiss watch exports were only worth half of their 1974 figure.

Interestingly, the story does not end there. In a marketing coup, the Swiss later invented the 'Swatch' brand – cheap timepieces that were effectively considered disposable fashion items. This was a new market, and the Swiss were... early adopters. They simultaneously began to revive more traditional analogue watches, selling them with an image based on history and tradition with little reference to the actual accuracy of the watch. Again, they were the first to adopt a unique and new market.

In the mid-1990s, I was working for a large Anglican church in Southampton. We were trying several evangelistic strategies to reach out to our local community. Much of our thinking had been traditional, sometimes spending 18 months (and several thousand pounds) building up to a 'mission week' with a speaker and a range of events. These were increasingly unsuccessful and, to be honest, a little demoralising at times. However, our mission work had included regularly running a course for those prepared to commit to exploring faith. There was nothing wrong with the course itself, but we felt somehow jaded and lacklustre about continuing. We had heard about a new-fangled course called 'Alpha', promoted from a big London church called Holy Trinity, Brompton (HTB) – and we decided to give it a go.

This was not a straightforward decision. The relative 'failure' of some of our activities had sapped our appetite for taking risks. The existing discipleship course might have been conservative, but we knew it worked. It would have been easy to say, 'Let's wait and see how this new course works in other churches.' In practice, on our very first Alpha course, six people came to real expressions of faith and we never looked back. With hindsight we were perhaps not 'early adopters', but certainly in the 'early majority' category. Alpha became a major tool in our evangelistic strategy.

Some of the detail here is important. We had not run an Alpha course before, but we had run something very similar, so the jump was much smaller for us than other churches. We were also an Anglican parish so the denominational connection with HTB gave it a sense of safety and security.

Diffusion of innovation is a brilliant theory, allowing us in real time to make judgments about strategic choices. Crucially it illustrates the importance of the 'fourth dimension' – time – that it matters not just that we make the right decision, but that *when* we make it is just as crucial.

CHAPTER 6:
SWOT

SWOTing up for great results

*I have Asperger's syndrome and that means
I'm sometimes a bit different from the norm.
And – given the right circumstances – being
different is a superpower.*

Greta Thunberg[1]

Like Handy's sine curve (which we'll explore more later), 'SWOT' can be
a great tool for the big strategic planning meetings. It is sometimes
attributed to Albert Humphrey, an American business and management
consultant (though he might have been building on the ideas of Franklin
Stewart at Stamford), but we do know that it has been a mainstream
leadership tool since the 1960s. We will consider its potential weaknesses
later, but it certainly deserves its place in the toolbox of every
organisation. One of the strengths of SWOT analysis is that it is almost
universally applicable and valuable – from a small-scale charity to a giant
multinational corporation. So, lets 'swot up' on how it works...

Bible stories

Numbers 13:1–3,17–20

The LORD said to Moses, 'Send some men to explore the land of Canaan,
which I am giving to the Israelites. From each ancestral tribe send one of
its leaders.'

So at the LORD's command Moses sent them out from the Desert of
Paran. All of them were leaders of the Israelites. [...] When Moses sent

them to explore Canaan, he said, 'Go up through the Negev and on into the hill country. See what the land is like and whether the people who live there are strong or weak, few or many. What kind of land do they live in? Is it good or bad? What kind of towns do they live in? Are they unwalled or fortified? How is the soil? Is it fertile or poor? Are there trees in it or not? Do your best to bring back some of the fruit of the land.' (It was the season for the first ripe grapes.)

The book of Numbers might as well be subtitled 'The Desert Years'. God's people are at a crucial turning point: rescued from Egypt, they are a nomadic set of tribes, wandering in the desert but clinging to the hope and promise of their own land. Like any promise from God, its fulfilment needs to be grasped, but in the right way and time. The whole chapter of Numbers 13 is an intriguing mix of the human and the divine. God has promised success and conquest, but is this the place, the time, and the way? Moses decides to hedge his bets with a bit of research. Is this land worth fighting for? What and who is there? God may be on their side but, humanly speaking, what will be the cost of conquest?

Nehemiah 2:11–16

I went to Jerusalem, and after staying there three days I set out during the night with a few others. I had not told anyone what my God had put in my heart to do for Jerusalem. There were no mounts with me except the one I was riding on. By night I went out through the Valley Gate toward the Jackal Well and the Dung Gate, examining the walls of Jerusalem, which had been broken down, and its gates, which had been destroyed by fire. Then I moved on toward the Fountain Gate and the King's Pool, but there was not enough room for my mount to get through; so I went up the valley by night, examining the wall. Finally, I turned back and re-entered through the Valley Gate. The officials did not know where I had gone or what I was doing, because as yet I had said nothing to the Jews or the priests or nobles or officials or any others who would be doing the work.

The story of Nehemiah is so much more than the famous rebuilding of the walls. Set at the other end of the story of the Old Testament from Moses, it is the story of God restoring His people to worship after the Babylonian captivity and exile. Restoration does however require some level of security, civic pride, and identity – so Nehemiah starts with the walls, but can he really achieve the task?

The theory

Like all the best tools, SWOT is fundamentally simple. We need to be mindful, however, that its simplicity may hide potentially rich areas of subtlety and depth. A SWOT (Strengths, Weaknesses, Opportunities, Threats) analysis is a way of enabling any organisation to step back and examine itself with a view to deciding future strategy. SWOT forces a more objective look than is possible when executives are engaged in the day-to-day running of their organisation. It will shine a light on factors that may otherwise be taken for granted and is best done by a diverse range of people from within the organisation who are able to bring a variety of perspectives and insights.

It is no accident that SWOT analyses are invariably produced and presented on a four-part matrix. A common way to do this might be to offer a blank matrix to your group (or divide a larger group of people into small groups) and get them to address each section for a short time (say, 10–15 minutes), pooling and collating the results. Practically, this might be done by offering sheets of flip-chart paper with a blank matrix and a marker pen. It is as basic as that!

Traditionally, strengths and weaknesses tend to be seen as internal factors, with opportunities and threats seen as external factors – but these definitions are not exclusive.

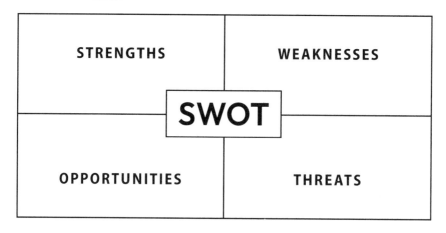

Strengths: These include things you do well, particularly if they distinguish you from your 'competition'. This might include products, modes of delivery, people, technical systems and service levels. Examples in the corporate world may be easy to think of; examples in ministry contexts may be harder, but might include a well-established Alpha course or great youth work. Strengths may be tangible or intangible, and the latter are easy to miss. This might include a mature and high-performing team, great links and relationships (trust) with outside bodies, or a unique approach to a task. Anything that can be defined as a USP (unique selling point/proposition) is by definition a strength. Once you start thinking, it is easy to see how the greatest strengths may not be the most obvious things, so it's vital to spend some time reflecting on and teasing out what they are. Like individuals, organisations tend to take for granted, and therefore under-appreciate, major strengths. Note also that any strength needs to be something that distinguishes you from others. You may have a great 'product', but if your competitors also produce a great product, this is not a strength but a necessity. Another interesting way of facilitating this part of the discussion is to hypothetically ask, 'What would our competitors say is our strength?'

Weaknesses: It's best to maintain a healthy awareness of weaknesses – and more often than not it's the people *not* in leadership roles who will be the most conscious of what these are. So don't be afraid to ask your staff/team! Weaknesses might include an inferior product that is outperformed by a rival, a dysfunctional individual or team, inability to recruit or retain staff or obviously poor decisions made at a strategic level in the past. Weaknesses may often be a component of a bigger picture – such as a great product but a poor order/delivery service, or a great product but poor after-sales support.

Opportunities: Depending on your context this might include technological developments that you can use to your advantage (adoption of web-based technology by virtually all organisations in the last 30 years is a great example here). External factors might also accelerate growth – perhaps if your local area is expanding with new housing estates, you may have an influx of new 'customers' to your church, college, or business. Again, opportunities may be tangible or quite abstract, and some will require some level of imagination and inspiration to be perceived. As uncomfortable as it may be to admit, opportunities may also arise due to problems at (or even the demise of) one of your 'competitors'. Many of us in ministry will have seen believers transfer their allegiance (and 'giving'), as a once thriving church struggles with internal problems. A recent example might be the exponential growth seen by renewable energy companies as climate change forces rapid technological change.

Threats: Threats will nearly always involve some level of *change* to the environment within which you are working. This might be sudden and catastrophic (perhaps your technology is compromised, or a key supplier goes bankrupt), but threats will often be much more understated. I have worked with several UK-based charities whose giving income has steadily declined as church attendance has itself declined. The change is slow but predictable and, unless some action is taken, the downward trend will continue. Threats and opportunities can present themselves either to individuals or the organisation (or both). It's also worth considering how individual personalities will engage with the SWOT process so, for example, those who are conflict-averse may find threats difficult to recognise or accept.

On paper, SWOT is beautifully simple. What could be more logical, rational and reasonable? In practice, most of the issues we need to consider stem from SWOT being utilised by humans who are frequently not logical, rational or reasonable. So it is worth noting some of the strengths and weaknesses of SWOT itself.

Anyone who has participated in a group SWOT exercise will recognise the simplicity but also the possibility of real depth in the process. Many factors will be subtle, not immediately recognised and may come from quieter members of the team. Some factors are hard to define. In a corporate context you may have a great product that is highly profitable (S) but also has a fragile supply chain (W/T). It is not uncommon to have additional dotted lines linking factors in two categories. SWOT provides material to consider, but doesn't necessarily offer any solution to problems or any inherent sense of priority. The material produced is highly dependent on who is there and their perspective. The process itself requires that potentially complex ideas are reduced to a short sentence or bullet point.

Depending on the team, examining weaknesses can be very challenging and, at times, personal. I attended one SWOT exercise in a training organisation which failed because the CEO refused to really engage with the idea of weakness, eventually magnificently sabotaging his own strategy day by declaring, 'Guys, we get enough criticism of what we do from people outside – I don't need any negativity here.' The implication really was, 'We're good, stay on message! Don't admit to weakness or rock the boat.' Any reflective process requires total honesty or it just won't work – and this may require strong leadership in the SWOT exercise itself. History teaches us that organisations that don't face and address their weaknesses now will be forced to address them later, with a much smaller chance of success. As Niccolo Machiavelli said, 'The wise man does at once what the fool does finally.'[2]

The very nature of SWOT can encourage 'group think'[3] where an idea is adopted, promoted, and celebrated. This does not mean it is a good idea or a correct perception of the way things are.

The SWOT process itself is vulnerable to strong and dominant characters who can make a good case for their pet project, and susceptible to what I call 'trump' (or 'sacred cow') products and policies – an innate belief that, whatever the cost, the organisation *must* do or produce something. There is also an argument that SWOT should be done regularly – few organisations can predict a pandemic or war which might have a major impact.

All of these considerations reinforce the point that to lead a SWOT analysis well is a real skill, and may well require a creative approach. For example, some sort of written, anonymous input may be required to diminish the dominance of the strong voices. It is certainly worth putting a lot of thought into the best way to ensure all voices are heard. Another creative process (stolen from 'listening skills' courses, and vital in conflict resolution) is to get individuals to reflect back and express someone else's perspective and opinion, not just their own.

There is also the danger (particularly in more bureaucratic organisations) of the SWOT analysis becoming an end in itself, when the real question at every end of a SWOT process is, 'What are we *going* to do?' The analysis demands some pretty hard negotiating and planning around strategic options brought up during the discussion. It should show you what work you have yet to do!

Finally, despite its simplicity and popularity, SWOT does have limitations. More modern (but similar) analyses include PEST (Political, Economic, Social and Technological) and its successor, PESTLE which also explores Legal and Environmental factors. These more highly developed tools tend to be particularly relevant in larger, more corporate contexts. One consultant suggested to me that you could do a SWOT analysis within each section of PEST or PESTLE, though there is then the severe danger of 'paralysis by analysis'.

Back to scripture

Numbers 13:25–33

At the end of forty days they returned from exploring the land.

They came back to Moses and Aaron and the whole Israelite community at Kadesh in the Desert of Paran. There they reported to them and to the whole assembly and showed them the fruit of the land. They gave Moses this account: 'We went into the land to which you sent us, and it does flow with milk and honey! Here is its fruit. But the people who live there are powerful, and the cities are fortified and very large. We even saw descendants of Anak there. The Amalekites live in the Negev; the Hittites, Jebusites and Amorites live in the hill country; and the Canaanites live near the sea and along the Jordan.'

Then Caleb silenced the people before Moses and said, 'We should go up and take possession of the land, for we can certainly do it.'

But the men who had gone up with him said, 'We can't attack those people; they are stronger than we are.' And they spread among the Israelites a bad report about the land they had explored. They said, 'The land we explored devours those living in it. All the people we saw there are of great size. We saw the Nephilim there (the descendants of Anak come from the Nephilim). We seemed like grasshoppers in our own eyes, and we looked the same to them.'

Moses and the people have never heard of SWOT but manage to do a pretty good job of utilising it as an approach! Arguably verses 17–20 are an invitation to do a clinical analysis of the land in SWOT terms. In the best tradition of SWOT, Moses selects a representative range of people, one from each of the 12 tribes.

Strength: In verse 30, Caleb declares, 'We should... take possession of the land, we can certainly do it.' It is a declaration of their strength. With God on their side, they have the power to do it, fulfilling destiny and God's promised plan.

Weakness: Verse 31 is the alternative and diametrically opposite view, 'they are stronger than we are... [the land] devours those living in it.'

Opportunities: The land 'flows with milk and honey' (v27). The two men have brought concrete evidence of this in a giant cluster of grapes. Imagine the attraction of this to the group still on the desert side of the Jordan!

Threats: To be fair to Caleb, his report is balanced, noting the threat of the well-established and fortified cities of the indigenous population.

Intriguingly, the debate continues in the next chapter with further suggestions of threat (the 'sword' and risk of enslavement in verse 3), and the oft-considered opportunity of returning to captivity in Egypt. We have noted that a SWOT analysis is never an end in itself and, in this story, the strategic decision to delay invasion is catastrophic. The people's lack of trust in God's plan for them results in this generation being banished to wander the desert for another 40 years. It is their children who will finally inherit the land.

> ### Nehemiah 4:6–10
> So we rebuilt the wall till all of it reached half its height, for the people worked with all their heart. But when Sanballat, Tobiah, the Arabs, the Ammonites and the people of Ashdod heard that the repairs to Jerusalem's walls had gone ahead and that the gaps were being closed, they were very angry. They all plotted together to come and fight against Jerusalem and stir up trouble against it. But we prayed to our God and posted a guard day and night to meet this threat. Meanwhile, the people in Judah said, 'The strength of the labourers is giving out, and there is so much rubble that we cannot rebuild the wall.'

The SWOT pattern is perhaps slightly less clear in Nehemiah; nevertheless, all the component parts are evident.

Strengths: It is clear from the narrative that much of the wall is still intact, so the task is more about repair than building from scratch. If ever a story is about leadership and the belief engendered by inspiring leadership, this is it. Nehemiah 4:10 notes the physical strength of the teams diminishing as the task is completed but the latent ability is clearly there at the start.

Weaknesses: The flipside to this is the tendency to lack self-belief – and it is played on by Nehemiah's enemies. Earlier, in Nehemiah 4:1, they mock the 'feeble Jews', and in 4:3 mock the wall itself, 'even a fox could break down their wall'. It is interesting that Sanballat and Tobiah identify this lack of confidence as a vulnerability in the project.

Threats: Throughout the project Sanballat, Tobiah and other non-Jews consistently oppose the building. The opposition starts as mocking and plots to fight in chapter 4, but by chapter 6 has become a complex and involved scheme to politically discredit Nehemiah, and possibly even assassinate him. In chapter 5, the unequal distribution of wealth and resulting poverty is identified as a real threat to the continued rebuilding.

Opportunities: Nehemiah is a master of motivation. A recurring skill of his is to motivate property owners to rebuild the section of wall next to their own residences (see Neh. 3:23 and Neh. 28). Self-interest can be harnessed as a strong motivator! It is also apparent that despite the run-down nature of Jerusalem, there is still enough military strength to provide protection whilst building. In fact, Nehemiah develops a hybrid soldier/builder (4:16–18). Above all, Nehemiah has identified the people's ability to respond to the need and his leadership. Progress is remarkable and the enthusiasm palpable.

Critics of SWOT may condemn it as little more than applied common sense, but the reality is that we need structured ways of appropriating common sense – it may prove more elusive and less common than we would like to think! Even Jesus (in a different context considering the cost of discipleship – see Luke 14:32) recommends a realistic appraisal of one's own strength and weakness compared to an enemy. The story of Nehemiah is a classic case of making the implicit, explicit: 'We didn't know we could do this... but we have.' Sometimes a theory's biggest strength is to help us own what we already implicitly knew but could not articulate. I emphasise again that SWOT is invariably only the beginning... the real question is, what are we going to do with it?

And finally...

I once applied for a job with a large UK-based charity working globally for poverty relief. I didn't get the job, but I remember chatting to the CEO over lunch where I asked what his major strategic priority was. Without hesitation he replied, 'To reduce the average age of our donors by ten years.' They had realised that a major threat to the organisation was the ageing of the donor base. The middle-aged folk that they had were generous givers (S), but they could not see a new generation of younger givers coming forward; if nothing changed, all the projections for income indicated a slow decline and death (T). The charity had some other enormous strengths including its spread across the country, a long history, great reputation, respect and strong professional image and communication skills. The clarity of the CEO's thinking was admirable in the light of this and clearly a response to a previous analysis of strengths and weaknesses.

Interestingly, on several occasions I have found myself working with other charities and organisations facing the exact same issue. Another response (opportunity) to this threat is to encourage charities to address legacies and wills. Donors may not be able to continue giving to the same extent as they age and are reliant on pensions, but they will (to be blunt) one day die. Legacies in wills may be dismissed as 'jam tomorrow' and have a level of uncertainty, but they can also have a substantial impact. Once a 'pipeline' of legacies is established, it can become a major strength of the organisation. This is the perfect example of something (in this case an ageing donor base) that might appear in both the 'threat' and 'opportunity' box of the SWOT analysis, and shows the complexity and breadth possible with the model.

CHAPTER 7: WICKED PROBLEMS

Big challenges and how not to solve them

A new type of thinking is essential if mankind is to survive and move toward higher levels.

Albert Einstein[1]

A friend of mine spent years working as a school nurse and was well used to the repetitive nature of team meeting agendas – the same issues, the same young people, the same organisations getting in the way. Eventually she quit, took a sabbatical year, and travelled around Africa in a Land Rover. To her surprise, on returning to the UK she found her job was being held open for her. But even after all that time away, she returned to find... yes, you guessed it: the agenda was *still* dominated by the same unsolved issues and, in many cases, the same young people and organisations! Other substantial issues had come and gone during her absence but there seemed to be an indefinable quality about some specific concerns that left them unresolved even after huge amounts of time, effort and ingenuity had been expended. What was going on?

The concept of 'wicked problems' is all down to a conversation between a number of management scientists (specifically Rittel, Churchman and Webber) working in the 1970s. Incidentally, 'wicked' has nothing to do with evil here – it is a *technical* description. Many problems are 'tame' – they may be tough, real problems, but they have a solution. Say, for example, you get ill with a bacterial infection. You are genuinely very ill, but we can fix that – a course of antibiotics will follow a predictable trajectory and you will get better. It's a tame problem. Wicked problems, by contrast, have a range of contradictory and complex aspects that make them much, much harder to fix.

Students of history will be aware of the Ancient Greek legend of the Gordian Knot. Discovered by Alexander the Great in 333 BC, the knot tethered a cart belonging to the founder of the capital city of Phrygia. Legend had it that he who untied the knot would go on to conquer Asia. Accounts vary, but the later ones have the hero applauded for simply slicing through the ball of rope with his sword. Wicked problems are (pardon the pun) 'knot' that simple.

In many ways, the whole of the book of Ecclesiastes is an extended essay on some wicked problems. As David Gibson says in his commentary, 'No one will finally come up with a solution to world poverty, or to all forms of injustice... so are we all doomed? Should we shut up shop and go home?'[2]

Of course, the answer is, no! Let's consider two very different biblical examples of engaging wicked problems.

Bible stories

Esther 3:8–11,13

Then Haman said to King Xerxes, 'There is a certain people dispersed among the peoples in all the provinces of your kingdom who keep themselves separate. Their customs are different from those of all other people, and they do not obey the king's laws; it is not in the king's best interest to tolerate them. If it pleases the king, let a decree be issued to destroy them, and I will give ten thousand talents of silver to the king's administrators for the royal treasury.'

So the king took his signet ring from his finger and gave it to Haman son of Hammedatha, the Agagite, the enemy of the Jews. 'Keep the money,' the king said to Haman, 'and do with the people as you please.' [...] Dispatches were sent by couriers to all the king's provinces with the order to destroy, kill and annihilate all the Jews – young and old, women and children – on a single day, the thirteenth day of the twelfth month, the month of Adar, and to plunder their goods.

The story of Esther is packed with drama. A complex plot sets up real jeopardy. Haman (the almost comically vain villain) has been insulted by Mordecai, who refuses to pay homage to a buffoon. Haman is a dangerous man, but unlike Haman, we know that Mordecai's adopted daughter Esther is now King Xerxes' favourite. Can she do something? We sense hope in the narrative, but the powerful language resonates down the centuries. Antisemitism is real, and we read this story today in the shadow of the Holocaust.

Romans 7:14–24

We know that the law is spiritual; but I am unspiritual, sold as a slave to sin. I do not understand what I do. For what I want to do I do not do, but what I hate I do. And if I do what I do not want to do, I agree that the law is good. As it is, it is no longer I myself who do it, but it is sin living in me. For I know that good itself does not dwell in me, that is, in my sinful nature. For I have the desire to do what is good, but I cannot carry it out. For I do not do the good I want to do, but the evil I do not want to do – this I keep on doing. Now if I do what I do not want to do, it is no longer I who do it, but it is sin living in me that does it.

So I find this law at work: Although I want to do good, evil is right there with me. For in my inner being I delight in God's law; but I see another law at work in me, waging war against the law of my mind and making me a prisoner of the law of sin at work within me. What a wretched man I am! Who will rescue me from this body that is subject to death?

This really is one of the great Pauline monologues on our intrinsic human failing – and the torment of trying to do what is right while finding ourselves inexorably driven by our inner nature to do wrong. Paul wrestles with his own internal conflict and ends with the rhetorical question, 'Who will rescue me?'

The theory

Ironically, it's a bit of a challenge to write about wicked problems. Most of the theories and tools in this book are popular because they offer at least some sort of answer to a problem. Whether providing a neat answer or just a clearer way to think about an issue, they generally bring at least some sort of intellectual satisfaction. Wicked problems are an exercise in learning to continue to struggle with what may seem almost insuperable challenges, while still believing that it is worth persevering, and a solution may eventually appear.

Rittel and Webber's observations of wicked problem characteristics include several specific characteristics:

- First, as hinted above, there is no simple, definitive formula to explain a wicked problem.

- Wicked problems have no 'stopping rule'. There is no way of knowing if your 'solution' is a definitive fix. To use a medical example, I mentioned earlier the use of antibiotics as a fix to the tame problem of a bacterial infection. By contrast, many medical interventions may only give an uncertain and potentially temporary respite from a chronic, long-term condition.

- Solutions to wicked problems are not 'true' or 'false' – they are simply good or bad, or (usually) some combination of the two.

- You cannot immediately test a solution to a wicked problem. We are used to the idea of 'modelling' solutions to problems (which may be possible with a wicked problem), but small-scale testing is not an option. Therefore every solution to a wicked problem is a one-shot operation; we cannot learn by trial or error, and every attempt counts significantly.

- Wicked problems are essentially unique, whereas tame problems tend to be variations of a similar problem that we have faced before.

- Every wicked problem is: a symptom of another problem; connected with another problem; or a result of another problem. Whilst Rittel and Webber did not specifically talk about 'secondary effects', there is an obvious link to this modern way of thinking about problem solving.

- Analysing, explaining, and making wicked problems comprehensible is difficult in itself because there will be more than one explanation of a wicked problem, and those explanations will in turn vary according to an individual's perspective.

- Those responsible for fixing the wicked problem may have no 'right to be wrong', and may be considered fully responsible for any outcome arising from their actions. Again, whilst Ritter and Webber did not consider this in depth, there is a specific link to organisational culture here – are risks encouraged, or is there a tendency to scapegoat when things don't work?

It is a moot point as to whether every wicked problem should feature every one of these characteristics but, by definition, wicked problems are not easy to define or categorise. In December 2019, a 61-year-old man made his regular visit to his local fish market in Wuhan, China. By the end of January, he was dead – the first victim of what become known globally as the Covid-19 pandemic. At least a further 80 million people fell sick with the coronavirus, and several millions have died.

Covid is an almost perfect example of a wicked problem. There is no definitive formula for a solution. Eradicating the virus is very imprecise, and required national governments to balance the risk of infection against the economic damage of multiple lockdowns, without any precedents by which to measure progress. Covid required a global solution, yet individual governments only had jurisdiction over their own territory and there was no comprehensive mechanism for agreeing or implementing a global response. Whilst pandemics had been modelled historically, this was the first time our world had faced a global pandemic in living memory. Many of the governments trying to manage Covid were democratically elected and conscious of the need to balance unpopular decisions against the desire to be seen to be successful.

Although vaccines have helped to restore some semblance of normal life, we may never totally eradicate the virus which mutates to thwart these efforts anyway. We can limit the spread of infection by quarantining people, but this can bring economic problems in its wake, as well as implications for mental, emotional and relational health. Regardless of our political affiliations, not many of us would relish the responsibility of trying to fix this!

Aside from Earth's seemingly permanent state of international crisis, we will all face wicked problems in life, business and ministry. So what are the insights we need to grasp?

First, the whole concept of wicked problems is gaining traction in culture, so if you are sitting in a multi-agency meeting with other professionals and this phrase is used, now you'll know what's going on. Second, the typology of 'simple', 'tame', and 'wicked' problems gives us a vocabulary in discussing issues. It doesn't matter how much positive thinking you get from your coach or how much your boss demands 'solutions, not problems!' – some issues are just super tough and super complex. 'Wicked' gives us a way of talking about this. Third, this vocabulary gives us a way of challenging the dialogue around some problems. Put simply, some problems will be labelled 'wicked' because people or organisations don't want to tackle them.

Back to scripture

Esther 7:1–6

So the king and Haman went to Queen Esther's banquet, and as they were drinking wine on the second day, the king again asked, 'Queen Esther, what is your petition? It will be given you. What is your request? Even up to half the kingdom, it will be granted.'

Then Queen Esther answered, 'If I have found favour with you, Your Majesty, and if it pleases you, grant me my life – this is my petition. And spare my people – this is my request. For I and my people have been sold to be destroyed, killed and annihilated. If we had merely been sold as male and female slaves, I would have kept quiet, because no such distress would justify disturbing the king.'

King Xerxes asked Queen Esther, 'Who is he? Where is he – the man who has dared to do such a thing?' Esther said, 'An adversary and enemy! This vile Haman!'

Then Haman was terrified before the king and queen.

I just love the complexity of this story and the way each turn of the plot is saturated in irony. King Xerxes is a bit of a people pleaser and readily agrees to Haman's revenge plan of genocide for the Jews. The new queen Esther can of course appeal to her husband to fix the problem... but he is the one who caused it (a frequent aspect of wicked problems), and she is of course Jewish, and therefore defined as part of the problem. The appeal to the king carries massive risk of causing offence (he will have to take a side) and is definitely a one-shot attempt at a fix. In the end, the story of Esther may seem like it has a definitive 'fix', but of course Jewish persecution has never really gone away.

Romans 7:25
Thanks be to God, who delivers me through Jesus Christ our Lord! So then, I myself in my mind am a slave to God's law, but in my sinful nature a slave to the law of sin.

Sin really is a genuine wicked problem – a symptom of our inner brokenness and rebellion with God. We don't believe we will ever find a 'stopping rule' this side of heaven, despite the reality of redemption and sanctification through Jesus. We may be inspired by the concept of Wesleyan holiness[3] but know it will only ever be partial. I love how *The Message* paraphrases Paul's answer to his own 'who will save me?' question:

The answer, thank God, is that Jesus Christ can and does. He acted to set things right in this life of contradictions where I want to serve God with all my heart and mind, but am pulled by the influence of sin to do something totally different.

And finally...

Wicked problems can be a litmus test of the quality of leadership in an organisation. The writer of Ecclesiastes observes, 'Fools are put in many high positions, while the rich occupy the low ones' (Eccl. 10:6). This is a classic wicked problem. No organisation can go beyond its own leader, and if the leader is too poor to be aware of their own weaknesses, the organisation is in trouble. The person to fix poor leadership is... the leader! Few leaders actually fire themselves, and most simply store up problems by trying to cover up their own weaknesses and mistakes. 'The first method for estimating the intelligence of a ruler,' observes Machiavelli, 'Is to look at the men he has around him.' Many organisations are held back by leaders who feel threatened by those who could help them.

There is a real danger that the whole concept of wicked problems can lead to an unjustified sense of acceptance. The concept of wicked problems might make us uncomfortable in that no amount of positive thinking or clever, upbeat strategy can necessarily bring a solution. Wicked problems are an exercise in accepting the long-term struggle necessary in many contexts.

Scripture, however (and especially the story of Esther), gives a uniquely faith-based perspective. Academics and writers on wicked problems love to give macro examples, citing world poverty, pandemics, or global warming. But wicked problems are frequently on a much smaller scale. In my experience they may even include quite localised pastoral problems within a church fellowship or commercial enterprise. This leads us back to a key insight that is evident from Esther. The fact that we cannot 'solve' a wicked problem does not mean that we can (or should) do nothing. The famous line from Esther is of course in 4:14 where Mordecai discerns Esther's elevation to be the king's favourite 'for such a time as this.' Threat, jeopardy and oppression of God's people was and is nothing new. Likewise, the adoption of a beautiful young woman into the King's court is business as usual. What the narrator of Esther does is uniquely bring these facts together as God creatively works out His plan of rescue in a way that could not have humanly been seen with conventional wisdom.

The Rotherham child sex abuse scandal of the 1990s and early 2000s (in the UK) arguably had many features of a wicked problem. The chaotic lives of victims (and to an extent the perpetrators), made any simple fix impossible. The nature, scale, and longevity of the issue made it such a big problem; it became easier for agencies to ignore rather than address it. Every part of the process was clouded by other issues. Girls were seen as 'prostitutes' rather than victims. One social worker, who tried to address the racial aspect by pointing out that white girls were being systematically exploited by gangs of Pakistani-British men, was disciplined and sent on a corrective 'race awareness' educational course. Pakistani girls who had been exploited did not want crimes investigated because of the cultural shame and damage to their marriage prospects. After a certain point, virtually every agency involved (council, child protection, social workers, and police) had more to lose by the scandal being exposed and passively covered it up. White girls also resisted help as their families were under threat.

In all this, there did emerge one astonishing and heroic 'Esther' figure. Jayne Senior was a youth worker and manager of 'Risky Business', a project which worked with young women at risk of sexual exploitation. An archetypal whistle-blower, Jayne worked for over ten years to uncover both the abuse and the systematic covering up of crime. She eventually cooperated on a series of articles in *The Times* newspaper, which finally triggered the inquiry that exposed the scandal. Jayne was awarded an MBE honour in 2016 for her work.

Esther's story is both an encouragement and a warning to us. Wicked problems exist but are never an excuse for despair or acceptance. Individuals may not be able to solve them absolutely, but that does not mean we can do nothing – and the biblical clarion call is to do whatever we can.

CHAPTER 8: GROUP LIFE

Why your group may have a mind of its own

> '*Never doubt that a small group of thoughtful, committed citizens can change the world: indeed, it's the only thing that ever has.*'
> **Margaret Mead[1]**

Even if you work in a professional role that involves a lot of one-to-one time with individuals, I think it's fair to assume that most of us will know what it is to be a part of groups and teams. In most Christian ministry contexts, it has become a very normalised expectation that we will work with groups: Sunday school groups, youth groups, elders' groups, Bible study groups, small groups… Many of us will also have experience of working with groups in a corporate context – maybe a sales team, or a group built around a specific project.

Over the years I have spent quite a lot of time coaching teachers being promoted beyond the classroom and into leadership. In many ways this is the hardest step of all. They have been judged by their ability as individual teachers, getting great results from their students. Management suddenly means that they are no longer judged on this alone but will be judged increasingly by their ability to get the best out of their colleagues; the members of their team. This requires a huge cognitive shift in approach and requires a new set of skills they were never taught during their teacher training. For this reason, the tools we'll be looking at in this chapter and the next are some of the most important for middle management.

If you work consistently with any kind of group – whether it is a gang you meet on the street or the doctors in your practice – you will know the slightly unsettling experience of the group taking on a life of its own. Not only does it seem to develop its own characteristics, but these can vary from week to week, or session to session. Incidentally, it is worth noting that every time someone does or does not turn up, the nature or composition of the group changes. We all bring something to groups we belong to beyond our 'functional role'. Someone may be the group joker, someone always has a whacky idea and someone else is the peacemaker. We often underestimate how much difference it makes when the composition of your group or team changes. If you have a group of just ten people then, depending on who may or may not attend each time, the possible number of combinations is (I will do the maths for you) 1,023. It is not surprising that the feel of the group varies so much from week to week. A shift in composition means a shift in dynamics.

Some weeks the group may seem full of life and energy, and other weeks there is almost a collective sense of listlessness or quietness. Sometimes there will be evidence of long-term change – not just random changes over time, but a significant sense of development in the group dynamics. We may welcome this because of the work we are doing as leaders, but at times there can be a sense that the changes are outside of our control. What on earth is happening?

Way back in 1965, a psychological researcher called Bruce Tuckman started to try to explain the more long-term changes we see in the 'life' of a group. It is one of the most enduring models of group growth, and we'll take a look at it in this chapter. But first, as we like precision in language, let's clarify some definitions. All teams are groups, but not all groups are teams. Here we are taking a common definition that a *group* is two or more individuals brought together either by a social need or the organisation (think of that break-out group you were put in at a conference). In contrast, a *team* is a collection of people linked together around (and/or to achieve) a common objective, such as winning a sports event. Much of the managerial literature on Tuckman tends to assume we are looking at a team tackling a task, but the application of Tuckman's theory is potentially much wider than that. The premise of both war and disaster movies is often that of a disparate group of people who are thrown together but eventually become a great team. Groups can *become* teams, and teams can fall apart.

Bible stories

We are going to dip into four connected Gospel stories to start exploring this. What links these narratives is that they are parts of the apostleship journey that Jesus' closest friends and followers were on.

Mark 1:16–20

As Jesus walked beside the Sea of Galilee, he saw Simon and his brother Andrew casting a net into the lake, for they were fishermen. 'Come, follow me,' Jesus said, 'and I will send you out to fish for people.' At once they left their nets and followed him.

When he had gone a little farther, he saw James son of Zebedee and his brother John in a boat, preparing their nets. Without delay he called them, and they left their father Zebedee in the boat with the hired men and followed him.

Mark 3:13–18

Jesus went up on a mountainside and called to him those he wanted, and they came to him. He appointed twelve that they might be with him and that he might send them out to preach and to have authority to drive out demons. These are the twelve he appointed: Simon (to whom he gave the name Peter), James son of Zebedee and his brother John (to them he gave the name Boanerges, which means 'sons of thunder'), Andrew, Philip, Bartholomew, Matthew, Thomas, James son of Alphaeus, Thaddaeus, Simon the Zealot.

As always, Mark's narrative style is sparse on detail but pregnant with possibility. Clearly Jesus is the leader and group former, but what is the task or objective around which the group is formed? There is a sense of excitement. At this stage the Twelve sound like a relatively coherent group (only fishermen from one location are mentioned). The differences in personality and approach are lurking but yet to be revealed.

Mark 10:35–37,41–43

Then James and John, the sons of Zebedee, came to him. 'Teacher,' they said, 'we want you to do for us whatever we ask.'

'What do you want me to do for you?' he asked.

They replied, 'Let one of us sit at your right and the other at your left in your glory.' [...]

When the ten heard about this, they became indignant with James and John. Jesus called them together and said, 'You know that those who are regarded as rulers of the Gentiles lord it over them, and their high officials exercise authority over them. Not so with you. Instead, whoever wants to become great among you must be your servant...'

Theologians, challenged on the effectiveness of relatively uneducated fishermen, love to point out that whatever their background, the Twelve could be considered to have had the best theological education ever – can you really beat three years with Jesus? In light of this, this dialogue is borderline shocking. How can the disciples get it so wrong?

Luke 9:46–48

An argument started among the disciples as to which of them would be the greatest. Jesus, knowing their thoughts, took a little child and had him stand beside him. Then he said to them, 'Whoever welcomes this little child in my name welcomes me; and whoever welcomes me welcomes the one who sent me. For it is the one who is least among you all who is the greatest.'

It sounds like a similar story here; big egos are vying for a place. Maybe Jesus is still in His 'year of popularity' and human ambition is driving friction?

The theory

Based on widespread research, Tuckman proposes that groups (which, remember, may be a team or just a group) will inevitably go through four stages:

Forming: This encompasses all the unpredictability of the start of the life of the group. Members may not know each other well (or at all). There is a high degree of uncertainty about how the group will work and what different roles individuals will play. At this stage there will be a high degree of dependence on the leader who will need to set the tone, ground rules and processes of the group. You may have experienced the feelings that arise here on a training event, for example, when you find yourself in a new group. Major personality traits will be fuelling this – extraverts[2] enjoying new company whilst introverts perhaps find it stressful.

Storming: This stage is characterised by a higher level of trust between members as they begin to get to know each other, but there then follows a period of conflict as individuals test boundaries and vie for position within the group. Small cliques may form, and the group may well have to focus on its task or purpose to avoid being distracted by personal issues. Tuckman's theory has some subtlety and depth that is seldom recognised, perhaps because of its simplicity. The 'storming' is enabled because there is the embryonic sense of growing trust. Paradoxically, people may need some minimum level of security to feel safe enough to challenge each other. There can be potentially negative aspects to this that are seldom explored, including the recognition that in cases where the conflict cannot be resolved, people will probably leave.

Norming: Agreement, compromise and consensus slowly lead to a level of clarity as roles and responsibilities become established and accepted. Remember that these roles may be the official professional ones that people have (Head of Sales; Finance Officer), or more abstract roles (group comedian; group feeder). As it settles down, the group exhibits a good level of commitment, unity and good process in decision making. The groups shows its ability to reflect on how it works and develops. Leadership responsibility may be shared and delegated effectively with respect and acceptance of the leader. (If you are dealing with children, patients or anyone who is unaccountable, then this sense of the group taking responsibility may be lessened, but there will still be a sense of the group 'settling'.)

Performing: A mature group simply performs well at what it is trying to achieve – which may be no more profound than having fun and enjoying each other's company! The leader may only need to give light-touch guidance as the group achieves accepted tasks and objectives. Disagreements tend to be resolved amicably and quickly. The group has a high level of independence and autonomy and can address issues of relationship and process as it works. As noted at the start, high-performing teams can be deeply satisfying to be a part of and work within.

Tuckman himself later added a fifth stage, 'adjourning' or 'mourning', which is about managing the ending of a group. This is particularly relevant where it is known that a group will terminate – examples might be the conference discussion group that has been exceptionally good; a group set up specifically for a mission task; a corporate project that has come to completion; a summer camp that has ended. This stage is about closing the group well by acknowledging the emotional investment that people have made, so members can celebrate their achievements and relationships, acknowledge the sense of sadness and loss, whilst also consciously moving on to new things.

Tuckman's theory has no specifically spiritual content but has some very applicable insights for us as Christian professionals and leaders. Most of the value of Tuckman's theory is about recognising what is happening, to make visible the 'invisible'. Recognising it allows us to name it and perhaps even process it creatively to bring about the best outcomes. Let's explore this further.

First, groups take time to gel. It doesn't matter whether you have put together a dream team of football stars, musicians, engineers, or a mission group. It takes *time* for the group to work through the stages and to begin achieving anything. There are no shortcuts and there is no way to cleverly avoid this by selecting people who you assume will instantly form a great working rapport. A wise approach is to *build in* time to allow for this process to unfold before circumstances require the group or team to be performing at its optimum level. Sports, music and many other industries are littered with failed 'dream teams'.

Second (and I consider this a key insight), things may get worse before they get better! The storming stage can be very alarming for any leader. It may feel as if we have invested in the group or team and yet everything is going wrong. The lesson here is to stick with the process – far from going wrong, you may be on the cusp of everything going right. Remember that people require a minimum level of security to even engage with this stage: a team that is not working at all is more likely to be in sullen silence than barbed banter. Friction may well be a sign of progress.

Third, your role as a leader can change dramatically as the group develops. The first two stages require hands-on, directive leadership, when you'll need to set the tone, pace, and ground rules. As the group reaches the norming stage, it may need much less direct input (which may or may not be welcome to you!) and the final performing stage only needs a light touch – you are not required to micro-manage every stage of this process. Some level of self-reflection is vital here. Some of us enjoy providing a directive style of leadership and may relish the first two stages, and risk irritating their group as they over-manage the last two stages. Others who enjoy the bigger picture of leadership but don't 'do' detail may find the first stages challenging but enjoy the greater sense of independence as the group matures.

Fourth, the group may briefly return to storming and norming as it encounters change. An example of this might be where a significant number of members of a group change, creating an almost entirely new group (such as a children's group based on school years). Again, a professional approach recognises the potential and opportunity of this and builds in time to work through it.

Finally, it's healthy to recognise the emotional costs involved. If you can easily think of a great team that you once belonged to... you may still be in the mourning stage!

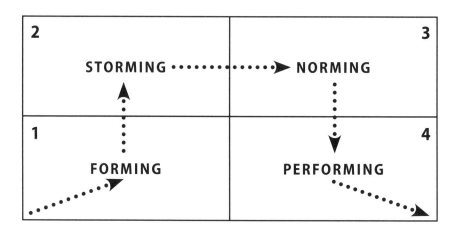

Remember, all 'tools' have weaknesses and limitations. Some observers are uncomfortable with the linear nature of Tuckman's model and question 'performing' as an end. Some Christians are uncomfortable with stage 2 (surely we'll just recognise our God-given gifts and get on with it?). But I would like to suggest that 'storming' will almost certainly happen in Christian groups – even if it is exhibited with subtlety and in the nicest possible way. Indeed, it may be harder to navigate this stage as we culturally find it difficult to process conflict.

Incidentally, it is an immutable law of small groups (popular in church) that if you do your job of leading well, the group is likely to grow. If it does, then depending on the context and policy of your organisation, it will either no longer be a small group (and you will lose the advantages of being a small group), or it will have to split, in which case you will inevitably face the 'adjourning' stage with its associated grief and loss, before embarking on a new round of 'forming' etc. This may not happen much in a corporate setting where teams are expensive and focused on a task, but is likely to be a common experience in a ministry setting which is more flexible.

Back to scripture

The two passages we've been considering from Mark 1 and 3 are a classic example of the 'forming' stage. The disciples might know each other a little, having lived in the same sort of area – but they don't know each other in the context of being a support group to a radical new, itinerant rabbi. They're also young, and their superficial knowledge might fool them that things are going to be easier than they are. It's therefore no surprise to find the disciples vying for position and status, but that's not the end of the story...

Luke 9:10,12–17

'When the apostles returned, they reported to Jesus what they had done. Then he took them with him and they withdrew by themselves to a town called Bethsaida [...] Late in the afternoon the Twelve came to him and said, 'Send the crowd away so they can go to the surrounding villages and countryside and find food and lodging, because we are in a remote place here.'

He replied, 'You give them something to eat.'

They answered, 'We have only five loaves of bread and two fish – unless we go and buy food for all this crowd.' (About five thousand men were there.)

But he said to his disciples, 'Have them sit down in groups of about fifty each.' The disciples did so, and everyone sat down. Taking the five loaves and the two fish and looking up to heaven, he gave thanks and broke them. Then he gave them to the disciples to distribute to the people. They all ate and were satisfied, and the disciples picked up twelve basketfuls of broken pieces that were left over.

John 6:25–29

When they found him on the other side of the lake, they asked him, 'Rabbi, when did you get here?'

Jesus answered, 'Very truly I tell you, you are looking for me, not because you saw the signs I performed but because you ate the loaves and had your fill. Do not work for food that spoils, but for food that endures to eternal life, which the Son of Man will give you. For on him God the Father has placed his seal of approval.'

Then they asked him, 'What must we do to do the works God requires?'

Jesus answered, 'The work of God is this: to believe in the one he has sent.'

We don't know the exact chronology of the Gospel accounts, but it is quite likely that these events may have happened relatively early. Certainly, the group of disciples were able to be focused and effective. Norming is to be welcomed.

Luke 10:1–11,17

After this the Lord appointed seventy-two others and sent them two by two ahead of him to every town and place where he was about to go. He told them, 'The harvest is plentiful, but the workers are few. Ask the Lord of the harvest, therefore, to send out workers into his harvest field. Go! I am sending you out like lambs among wolves. Do not take a purse or bag or sandals; and do not greet anyone on the road. When you enter a house, first say, "Peace to this house." If someone who promotes peace is there, your peace will rest on them; if not, it will return to you. Stay there, eating and drinking whatever they give you, for the worker deserves his wages. Do not move around from house to house. When you enter a town and are welcomed, eat what is offered to you. Heal the sick who are there and tell them, "The kingdom of God has come near to you." But when you enter a town and are not welcomed, go into its streets and say, "Even the dust of your town we wipe from our feet as a warning to you. Yet be sure of this: The kingdom of God has come near."' [...] The seventy-two returned with joy and said, 'Lord, even the demons submit to us in your name.'

What a cracking passage! Frustratingly, Luke gives a lot of detail of the task briefing for the team, but almost no detail of what happened. From the last verse, things clearly went well, the disciples are buzzing and the performing stage has clearly been reached.

I believe in the importance of intellectual honesty so there is a big caveat here. The eagle-eyed amongst you will have noticed that these stories do not necessarily appear to come in the same order in the Gospel accounts as the Tuckman stages. They might, but let's remember that the Gospels have never claimed to be chronologically accurate and measured accounts of the life of Jesus. The point here is not to try to shoehorn Tuckman's model into scripture but simply to point out that with certain stimuli, any group is capable of evidencing any of Tuckman's stages of group development.)

So, Tuckman's theory is a classic – simple, memorable, and much used by professionals in many situations. If you are unfamiliar with it, think of a variety of new group situations you have been in and what behaviour was shown. Try to memorise the basic outline and go from there!

And finally...

A particularly rewarding part of my own career involved joining a new team designed to facilitate faith development within a Church of England diocese. It was a great project with decent funding, and the team had a good feel of dedicated people with a wealth of gifting and experience. I was one of two youth officers, covering different geographical areas. We knew each other vaguely and brought radically different approaches. She had lots of experience working on a disadvantaged estate doing and sustaining pioneering youth work where other agencies had simply failed; my experience was mostly with young people from more privileged backgrounds and on a large scale.

Things started well but our own relationship deteriorated quite quickly. I couldn't put my finger on what the problem was, and things soon soured to the point where she and I had a significant row on the phone one evening. My boss and team leader (with wit and wisdom) liked to refer to this afterwards as our 'spat'. Both my colleague and I quickly apologised, made up and generally worked well together from then on. The row was without doubt cathartic, and I suspect both sides needed to speak our truth and clear the air in order to move forward.

CHAPTER 9: TEAM MANAGEMENT

Nobody's perfect but a team can be

> *The lone helmsman, whatever his [sic] ability,
> is prone to mistakes and oversights which
> reflect the limitations of his knowledge and
> experience. The management team has
> become the stable alternative.*
> **Belbin**[1]

We are social beings. We love working together, and there is something deeply satisfying about the sense of achievement we get when we are dependent on others, especially when they too are reliant on the contribution we bring. Stephen Covey would define this as 'interdependence'[2] and sees it as a major goal in our working and personal relationships. And, as we read in Paul's epistles, it's a biblical principle too.

Recapping a key point from the previous chapter: all teams are groups, but not all groups are teams. Dr Raymond Meredith Belbin, a management consultant, focused his work around *teams* seeking to achieve a defined (commercial) goal. It's his model I'm going to talk about here – The Nine Belbin Team Roles – and explore how it is the role of the leader to identify, value and maximise all the different qualities that various personalities within your team are bringing to the table.

Bible stories

A recurring theme in Paul's writing was the need to recognise different talents within the Church for it to work effectively. Let's begin with two of his best-known passages, with a view to branching out a bit later.

Ephesians 4:7,11–13 (NLT)

However, he has given each one of us a special gift through the generosity of Christ. [...] Now these are the gifts Christ gave to the church: the apostles, the prophets, the evangelists, and the pastors and teachers. Their responsibility is to equip God's people to do his work and build up the church, the body of Christ. This will continue until we all come to such unity in our faith and knowledge of God's Son that we will be mature in the Lord, measuring up to the full and complete standard of Christ.

The context of this teaching is a call to unity within the church. The human assumption is that it is easy for diversity to lead to difference, and this seems to be on Paul's mind. It is a well-known tendency within the human resources profession to note that we tend to 'recruit in our own image', so middle-aged white men, when looking for a new work colleague, tend to recruit... middle-aged white men! But Paul is embracing diversity here.

Note that the gifts are described here in the context of God's grace. The acronym I was taught in youth group for this was 'Great Riches At Christ's Expense', which sums it up pretty well. It might be a bit of a stretch to talk of the Church – the body of Christ –as a 'team', but the underlying value in Paul's thinking is clearly compatible with Belbin's theory (which we will explore) that *strength lies in diversity and difference*. The best teams have variety and learn to overcome the inherent frictions that difference brings.

This theme is also famously expressed and explored by Paul in his letter to the Corinthians:

1 Corinthians 12:3–7,15–26 (NLT)

So I want you to know that no one speaking by the Spirit of God will curse Jesus, and no one can say Jesus is Lord, except by the Holy Spirit. There are different kinds of spiritual gifts, but the same Spirit is the source of them all. There are different kinds of service, but we serve the same Lord.

God works in different ways, but it is the same God who does the work in all of us. A spiritual gift is given to each of us so we can help each other. [...] If the foot says, "I am not a part of the body because I am not a hand," that does not make it any less a part of the body. And if the ear says, "I am not part of the body because I am not an eye," would that make it any less a part of the body? If the whole body were an eye, how would you hear? Or if your whole body were an ear, how would you smell anything? But our bodies have many parts, and God has put each part just where he wants it. How strange a body would be if it had only one part! Yes, there are many parts, but only one body. The eye can never say to the hand, "I don't need you." The head can't say to the feet, "I don't need you."

In fact, some parts of the body that seem weakest and least important are actually the most necessary. And the parts we regard as less honorable are those we clothe with the greatest care. So we carefully protect those parts that should not be seen, while the more honorable parts do not require this special care. So God has put the body together such that extra honor and care are given to those parts that have less dignity. This makes for harmony among the members, so that all the members care for each other. If one part suffers, all the parts suffer with it, and if one part is honored, all the parts are glad.

One of the biggest problems we face with this passage is our familiarity with it. Those who have lived and explored faith through the later movements of the Spirit in the twentieth century are programmed to a particular interpretation of Paul's words. Sermons we have heard tend to focus on the *gifting of the Spirit*. This is of course correct, but can also be a smoke screen to some of the more subtle points inherent in Paul's thinking. As with this passage from Ephesians, the real emphasis is on unity and working together both because of, and despite, difference.

Paul's metaphor could have ended at verse 12, but instead he embarks on an extended commentary that is longer than the metaphor itself. Note in verse 15 the danger of comparison. Some want gifts that they do not have, others do not appreciate the gifts given in certain people and again, there is the danger that gifts are unappreciated and undervalued.

Paul calls out our natural tendency to favour the gifts we see in attractive people (vv22–24). Gifts only come 'packaged' in a human being and our feelings for the person may cloud our judgment of their contribution overall.

The theory

How do we understand what is happening beneath the surface of our team and how might we make it function better? Belbin became famous for working with FTSE Top 100 corporate teams. Despite this elitist approach, his insights have become a major part of mainstream thinking and you will meet them in professional conversations. Belbin's famous quote was, 'Nobody's perfect but a team can be.'[3] Notwithstanding any theological qualms we might have (a team of sinners... perfect?), Belbin had two clear insights: the first was that a good team is more than the sum of its parts. A technical term for this is 'synergy'. We all bring something to the table, but the result can be extraordinarily good – indeed much better than expected. There are many examples of this in the sporting world, where teams of seemingly average players work together to beat teams dominated by, and built around, a couple of key superstar talents. There is a particular theological insight here in Paul's writing, since this famous passage on 'the body' is actually set in a narrative about *love*.

Belbin's second insight is crucial: whilst we all probably have a stated role in the team (chairperson; treasurer; safeguarding officer), we all also bring a *team role*.

Think about a team you know. You might find yourself saying something like, 'John is a good welcomer, Sally always brings creative ideas, Eric stops us wandering off into a fantasy land of great dreams and Laura checks we have done what we agreed to last month. Oh, and Mike brings great cakes.' Belbin's insight is to categorise and label these team roles – not our technical function but the invisible role we play in the team itself. These nine roles are:

- **Resource Investigator:** This might literally be someone who knows where to borrow a PA system but more generally means someone outgoing and good at developing and utilising contacts. They can occasionally be over-optimistic and lose enthusiasm after initial interest.

- **Teamworker:** These guys are good at not just doing the work but making sure the team itself works well. Good listeners, diplomatic, tactful, they can avoid confrontation and struggle with unpopular decisions.

- **Co-ordinator:** These stay focused on the big objective and delegate effectively to achieve it. Mature and confident, their delegation can be perceived as 'offloading' work.

- **Plant:** Highly creative and good at finding unconventional solutions to problems. Radical, creative, and free-thinking, they are not so good at detail and can be a bit absent-minded.

- **Monitor Evaluator:** Logical, impartial, and clinical in assessing a team's options. They are strategic and discerning but can be critical and lack drive.

- **Specialist:** What is says on the tin – they bring in-depth knowledge but only of a narrow area. They can be vital but can also get stuck on technicalities and overload you with detailed information.

- **Shaper:** These guys bring drive, focus and momentum to keep the team on task. They can be courageous, challenging and thrive on pressure, but can also be provocative and offend in their determination to get things done.

- **Implementer:** Unlike the shaper, these folk contribute to team efficiency by working out a strategy and carrying it out. They turn ideas into action through organisation, but like a big ship, can be slow to respond to new directions.

· **Completer Finisher:** Particularly important towards the end of a task or project, CFs like quality control, checking things are done and to a high standard. They are good on detail, conscientious and painstaking, but can also be perfectionists who worry and struggle to delegate.

There are two more insights to bring into the equation to help us get the most from this tool. First, you *do not* need one person with each quality on your team (phew!). Experience shows that most of us will bring at least two of the Belbin roles to any team we join. Nevertheless, your team is weakened if any role is clearly missing. Second, the importance of each role varies with the situation the team is in. Resource Investigators and Implementers are important at the start of a task or project; Shapers and Co-ordinators are important in the middle; and Completer Finishers are essential at the end. Reflective practitioners may be able to fulfil different roles in different team contexts depending on what is needed, though it always takes more energy to fill a role that does not come naturally to you.

Having said that, it is the overall balance of roles that matters. You can do online questionnaires to work out the Belbin role that you are most comfortable with but most of us can intuitively recognise what we have or lack in our team.[4] One of Belbin's key observations was that many corporate teams lacked a Plant (who is going to recruit a 'whacky ideas guy' to the board, especially that of a FTSE 100 company or a large, highly respected charity?) – but they suffered for the absence of this.

It's important to recognise whether our official role is easily compatible with our Belbin team role. I was once on a church staff team whose chair was, at his own admission a Plant – and a really good one! But, every week he brought a plateful of new ideas, and we inevitably got sidetracked. Generally speaking, a chairperson is more effective if they are a Shaper, Monitor Evaluator or Co-ordinator by nature.

So, have a look at your team in terms of Belbin roles. Who plays what role? If you don't want to do the official Belbin questionnaire, find a fun and engaging way of discussing the roles at a team meeting or retreat day. If you can recognise what you lack, how can you address that? If people's function does not match their Belbin role, what creative solutions can you come up with? There is, for example, no need for the boss to always chair team meetings.

Back to scripture

So many stories in scripture are brimming with God's creativity in bringing disparate people to work together for His Kingdom. There is always a danger with the Bible that we read into it what we want to find. You can make your own mind up, but I think we can find some pretty good Belbin examples! For starters, here are some suggestions (and yes, I had to include some of the disciples from the most famous team of all).

Resource Investigator

Genesis 30:29–30 (NLT)

Jacob replied, "You know how hard I've worked for you, and how your flocks and herds have grown under my care. You had little indeed before I came, but your wealth has increased enormously. The LORD has blessed you through everything I've done. But now, what about me? When can I start providing for my own family?"

Like him or not, Jacob is arguably one of the most enterprising characters in the Old Testament. Like a cat that falls on its feet, you can put Jacob into any situation, and he always seems to be able to charm his way to the top. On the run from a murderous brother in Genesis 29, he arrives in Paddan Aram. By the time he leaves his employer Laban 14 years later, he has snaffled both his daughters, several servants and most of his flocks of sheep and goats.

Teamworker

Acts 9:26–27 (NLT)

When Saul arrived in Jerusalem, he tried to meet with the believers, but they were all afraid of him. They did not believe he had truly become a

believer! Then Barnabas brought him to the apostles and told them how
Saul had seen the Lord on the way to Damascus and how the Lord had
spoken to Saul. He also told them that Saul had preached boldly in the
name of Jesus in Damascus.

I love Barnabas. He is generous (Acts 4:36), loyal to friends (Acts 9:26–27),
an encourager (Acts 11:22–26) and forgiving (Acts 15:36–41). Here we
read of how Paul, the converted and now highly driven Shaper, doesn't
have time for John-Mark's weaknesses. The whole team could have
disintegrated but instead Barnabas effectively says, 'Don't worry, I'll take
him,' and two brilliant teams emerge from the ashes of dispute.

Co-ordinator

Acts 6:1–5 (NLT)

In those days when the number of disciples was increasing, the
Hellenistic Jews among them complained against the Hebraic Jews
because their widows were being overlooked in the daily distribution of
food. So the Twelve gathered all the disciples together and said, "It would
not be right for us to neglect the ministry of the word of God in order
to wait on tables. Brothers and sisters, choose seven men from among
you who are known to be full of the Spirit and wisdom. We will turn this
responsibility over to them and will give our attention to prayer and the
ministry of the word." This proposal pleased the whole group.

We can commend the unknown disciple here. The apostles are getting
distracted from the main task of 'prayer and the ministry of the word' by
a dispute about food distribution amongst the community. Somebody
(we are never told their name) – but clearly a Co-ordinator who can stay
focused on the main task – speaks up and the dispute is resolved.

Plant

Matthew 14:22–23,25–29 (NLT)

Immediately after this, Jesus insisted that his disciples get back into the boat and cross to the other side of the lake, while he sent the people home. After sending them home, he went up into the hills by himself to pray. Night fell while he was there alone. [...] About three o'clock in the morning Jesus came toward them, walking on the water. When the disciples saw him walking on the water, they were terrified. In their fear, they cried out, "It's a ghost!" But Jesus spoke to them at once. "Don't be afraid," he said. "Take courage. I am here!" Then Peter called to him, "Lord, if it's really you, tell me to come to you, walking on the water." "Yes, come," Jesus said. So Peter went over the side of the boat and walked on the water toward Jesus.

Here Peter wins 'best Plant' by a mile. Walk on water? Yeah! Why not? Build some shelters? Great idea! Declare unconditional loyalty? No problem. Cut off someone's ear? – you get the picture. Peter is brilliant but spontaneous, crazy and enthusiastic... all at the same time. But Peter is not *just* spontaneous. Loyalty is a good thing, and being prepared to defend oneself is a good value. It is Peter's *combination* of these traits with the creativity of his thinking that is so distinctive.

Monitor Evaluator

Matthew 26:20–22,25 (NLT)

When it was evening, Jesus sat down at the table with the Twelve. While they were eating, he said, "I tell you the truth, one of you will betray me." Greatly distressed, each one asked in turn, "Am I the one, Lord?" [...] Judas, the one who would betray him, also asked, "Rabbi, am I the one?" And Jesus told him, "You have said it."

Just to show that there is neither moral condemnation nor recommendation in any role, we are going to consider Judas Iscariot here. Judas seems to have had a clinical, detached judgment which, particularly towards the end of Jesus' ministry, led him to discount Jesus as the sort of Messiah he thought he needed. His disillusionment seems to have been gradual over the three years, but by the end he decides that being treasurer (and pilfering the money – see John 12) is not enough. A full-scale desertion combined with a grand attempt to maximise his gains is the only logical option in Judas' mind. We may condemn him, but there is an evaluative drive to his decision making.

Specialist

Nehemiah 2:2–5,11–12,16–17 (NLT)

So the king asked me, "Why are you looking so sad? You don't look sick to me. You must be deeply troubled." Then I was terrified, but I replied, "Long live the king! How can I not be sad? For the city where my ancestors are buried is in ruins, and the gates have been destroyed by fire." The king asked, "Well, how can I help you?" With a prayer to the God of heaven, I replied, "If it please the king, and if you are pleased with me, your servant, send me to Judah to rebuild the city where my ancestors are buried." […] So I arrived in Jerusalem. Three days later, I slipped out during the night, taking only a few others with me. I had not told anyone about the plans God had put in my heart for Jerusalem. We took no pack animals with us except the donkey I was riding. […] The city officials did not know I had been out there or what I was doing, for I had not yet said anything to anyone about my plans. I had not yet spoken to the Jewish leaders—the priests, the nobles, the officials, or anyone else in the administration. But now I said to them, "You know very well what trouble we are in. Jerusalem lies in ruins, and its gates have been destroyed by fire. Let us rebuild the wall of Jerusalem and end this disgrace!"

Nehemiah gives the entirety of his next chapter to the literal nuts and bolts of rebuilding Jerusalem's walls and gates. They're a practical bunch and not surprisingly have the hands-on skills in abundance. What they lacked was motivation, which Nehemiah (clearly also a Shaper and Co-ordinator) brings. Ultimately the task is as much a spiritual one as a manual one, and at the end Ezra the priest and scribe is brought on to read the law to the returning Israelites.

Shaper

Acts 27:27,33,38,42–44 (NLT)

About midnight on the fourteenth night of the storm, as we were being driven across the Sea of Adria, the sailors sensed land was near. [...] Just as day was dawning, Paul urged everyone to eat. "You have been so worried that you haven't touched food for two weeks," he said. [...] After eating, the crew lightened the ship further by throwing the cargo of wheat overboard. [...] The soldiers wanted to kill the prisoners to make sure they didn't swim ashore and escape. But the commanding officer wanted to spare Paul, so he didn't let them carry out their plan. Then he ordered all who could swim to jump overboard first and make for land. The others held on to planks or debris from the broken ship. So everyone escaped safely to shore.

Here's another example of why I think Paul is brilliant. We tend to think of him as the great orator and church planter, the navigator of missionary journeys and the shaper of our grace-based theology. He is the archetype of a life turned around by encounter with Jesus. This narrative shows a radically different side of his character. In practical situations he keeps cool and motivated, calmly managing the fallout of a shipwreck disaster.

To add an intriguing thought about how God uses our gifts, it would be possible to make a case that Paul was a Shaper *before* his conversion.

Implementer

Genesis 41:46–49 (NLT)

[Joseph] was thirty years old when he began serving in the court of Pharaoh, the king of Egypt. And when Joseph left Pharaoh's presence, he inspected the entire land of Egypt. As predicted, for seven years the land produced bumper crops. During those years, Joseph gathered all the crops grown in Egypt and stored the grain from the surrounding fields in the cities. He piled up huge amounts of grain like sand on the seashore. Finally, he stopped keeping records because there was too much to measure.

The Joseph we read about in Genesis 41 is absolutely smashing it – not only in terms of character (and let's not overlook what he went through to get there) but, like Paul, he is also a fantastic manger and team leader. The account is pretty sparse: 'Joseph collected all the food in those seven years of abundance' (v48), but even without any further details offered, Joseph was clearly running highly professional and effective teams. The narrative thrust is to reflect on character, but this implementer successfully navigated a colossal logistical exercise, avoiding national famine and saving lives.

Completer Finisher

> ### Luke 10:38–42 (NLT)
> As Jesus and the disciples continued on their way to Jerusalem, they came to a certain village where a woman named Martha welcomed him into her home. Her sister, Mary, sat at the Lord's feet, listening to what he taught. But Martha was distracted [...] She came to Jesus and said, "Lord, doesn't it seem unfair to you that my sister just sits here while I do all the work? Tell her to come and help me." But the Lord said to her, "My dear Martha, you are worried and upset over all these details! There is only one thing worth being concerned about. Mary has discovered it, and it will not be taken away from her."

She often faces a lot of unfair criticism thanks to this passage, but fair play to Martha: she's a CF! Again, this is a reminder that all roles have inherent strengths and weaknesses. Martha is not a bad person for wanting to stay on task. But, in this context, she has mismanaged her priorities, and her attention to detail has prevented her from getting the most out of the situation.

And finally…

Do you remember the days when PE teachers made the students pick sports teams? Team captains would be selected, who then went on to choose those they wished to have on their teams. The system had its merits: if there were two excellent football players, for example, the sequential selection process would result in one being on each team. The method was eventually outlawed in most schools due to the humiliation imposed on those who were selected last, a public indictment and embarrassing verdict on their uselessness in that sport. But despite its flaws, this approach raises several real-life issues about teams. Selecting their players gave 'captains' a real sense of the importance and responsibility of team building. Good teams don't just happen, they require planning, reflection, and analysis. The system was also a lesson in the reality that what might look like a great team does not always function as such. One of the triggers to Belbin's extensive research was the repetitive finding that what looked like an alpha team of hot shots (he actually called them 'Apollo' teams), frequently performed spectacularly badly.

This raises another issue for many managers and leaders. To have the option to select a team from scratch is a rare privilege and is to be grasped as such. A far more common experience is to inherit a team someone else has developed (or not) over a much longer period of time. The chances are you may frequently be used as a trouble-shooter in a team that is clearly dysfunctional.

Belbin's work does need to come with a health warning. His theory originated in the corporate world where an apparent team defect could be remedied by hiring another well paid executive – an option that is seldom open to many of us in ministry, charity, military or many corporate contexts. As we've said, most of us will already play multiple roles on a team. The power of Belbin is in making us *aware* of what is going on and providing us with language we can use to address it. When we can understand why our team is not quite working as it should, we can at least start to remedy the situation. Equally, Belbin's theory can help us acknowledge that a mundane-looking team might actually be functioning very well. It is not about appearance but synergy, and many a good team has been broken up because decision makers didn't recognise the quality that was in front of them.

LEAD

CHAPTER 10:
ORGANISATIONAL CULTURE

Culture eats strategy for breakfast.
Peter Drucker[1]

Many years ago, in another life, I was a computer salesman in the early days of microcomputers. I was issued with the compulsory suit, portable computer and a Ford Mondeo and spent several years racing round the country selling to transport professionals. A regular experience (and you'll be familiar if you've ever worked in sales) was trying to work out who actually made the decisions in any organisation. There might have been several people in the room, but who really controlled what happened? Who did I need to influence?

On one occasion I was in the far North of Scotland (Banff to be precise), trying to sell to the local authority. We started the meeting with the usual formal introductions but, several minutes later as I was in full flow of my pitch, a rather casually dressed and shambling gentleman of mature years wandered in unannounced and sat in a back corner. As a basic professional courtesy, I included him in the 'lighthouse' sweeps of my presentation, but didn't give him much further attention. Much, much later, I discovered later that he was in fact the head of computing for the authority... most definitely someone who had the ability to approve or block the purchase. Thankfully, I did make the sale – but it was a clear reminder to me that appearances can be deceptive. It's always worth finding out what's really going on.

This chapter, I want to talk about organisational culture in light of research done by Charles Handy, a great leadership and management guru. One of Handy's main insights was that regardless of what organisational *structure* is presented on paper, any organisation (whether commercial, church, military or charity) has a *culture* of organisation.

Remember that we are defining culture as 'how we do things round here'; that set of expectations and traditions that have been established in any working context. Remember also, that these traditions, values, and expectations are generally more powerful for having not been written down! They're the things that everybody else seems to just *know*. We tend to be more anxious to discover these things when we are new to a place and want to fit in. Culture may well be presented as tradition, like, 'Oh, we always bring cakes in for the coffee break when it's our birthday.' But there may also be very powerful expectations around clothing, behaviour, deference and pecking order. It is not uncommon to find organisations where not only do the managers all look alike, but they also actually start to sound alike as well with adopted slang and mannerisms.

It is the *culture* that you will be dealing with, so you can avoid a lot of potential frustration by identifying what type of organisation is in front of you. I stress again, the *culture* may or may not resemble the ostensible *structure* of the organisation. The gatekeepers might not be who they think they are. The PA, not the CEO, might really be the one running the show.

Bible stories

We'll start by focusing on two New Testament examples, and broaden the consideration later in the chapter.

Matthew 2:1–5,7–8

After Jesus was born in Bethlehem in Judea, during the time of King Herod, Magi from the east came to Jerusalem and asked, 'Where is the one who has been born king of the Jews? We saw his star when it rose and have come to worship him.'

When King Herod heard this he was disturbed, and all Jerusalem with him. When he had called together all the people's chief priests and

teachers of the law, he asked them where the Messiah was to be born.
'In Bethlehem in Judea,' they replied. […]

Then Herod called the Magi secretly and found out from them the
exact time the star had appeared. He sent them to Bethlehem and said,
'Go and search carefully for the child. As soon as you find him, report to
me, so that I too may go and worship him.'

As is often the case, Matthew's narrative is sparse in detail but drops
some tantalising clues. The mysterious Magi arrive. Clearly they are
people of substance and wealth, for they get an audience with Herod –
or, perhaps in the best tradition of paranoid tyrants, any significant new
arrivals in the territory need to be checked out. Are they naive or being
provocative in asking the existing king where a new one might be?

Both Herod's kingship and his Roman citizenship were conferred on
him by the despised Roman occupiers. Whilst technically a practising
Jew, it is probably not surprising that his depth of faith did not extend to
knowing the predicted location of the long-awaited Messiah's birthplace
– this had to be ascertained from the chief priests. The life of Herod has
been documented in considerable detail by contemporary historians, and
the account of Jesus' birth comes in the latter stages of his reign when
he is descending into a barbaric and disorganised stage of government
(killing numerous members of his own family, including a wife he had
previously loved and his first-born son Antipater). At this point, Herod is a
ruthless and volatile despot whom no one dares to challenge.

Acts 25:9–11

Festus, wishing to do the Jews a favour, said to Paul, 'Are you willing to
go up to Jerusalem and stand trial before me there on these charges?'

Paul answered: 'I am now standing before Caesar's court, where I
ought to be tried. I have not done any wrong to the Jews, as you yourself
know very well. If, however, I am guilty of doing anything deserving
death, I do not refuse to die. But if the charges brought against me by
these Jews are not true, no one has the right to hand me over to them. I
appeal to Caesar!'

This conversation between Paul and local governor Porcius Festus is such a contrast to Herod's dialogue that it's hard to believe they were dealing with the same regime. There are fascinating similarities: Paul represented a growing religious sect that threatened to destabilise the locality, and was portrayed as such by the vested interests of Judaism – just as the birth of a new 'king' would destabilise Jerusalem in the time of Herod. By contrast, Festus is recorded as being a decent local ruler who played by the rules and was noted for his wisdom and honesty. Paul likewise plays it straight, drawing on the rights he has as a Roman citizen. How will either narrative end?

The theory

Charles Handy was the son of an Irish Archdeacon. He started his career at a giant oil company but eventually left to teach business in London. On the verge of great success, he returned to Ireland for his father's funeral. His perception of his father had been that of a rather timid and ineffectual priest, but Handy was astounded at the huge number of people who attended the funeral and the obvious impact of his ministry. This turned out to be a moment of epiphany for Charles, and led him to new ways of thinking around how capitalism and business can be harnessed for human flourishing. He is without doubt one of the most influential and creative thinkers, especially around the subject of understanding and working with organisations. His thinking is unusual in that it has encompassed the corporate world but especially that of voluntary organisations and educational institutions.

Handy's core thesis is to identify four types of organisational culture:

Power culture: Think of a spider sitting at the centre of a web. This organisation is really all about the leader, who makes decisions quickly. It is difficult to grow this kind of organisation: there is only one leader, who often becomes a vital gateway (all decisions must go through or be approved by them), and the organisation may fold if they leave. Power is at the centre and the nearer you get to the leader, the closer to real power you are. The organisation is judged by results.

Role culture: Think of a building with the roof held up by columns, each column representing a role (maybe HR, or Marketing), each taking some weight. Power is invested in the *position*, not the *person* (eg the HR Director is replaced if they leave). These organisations can be successful and stable but can be slow to perceive the need to change and respond to events. A good example might be a university or a large corporation.

Task culture: Think of a net or matrix where different strands intersect. This is a strong team culture based around achieving an objective and often drawing on different types of expertise (eg a multi-disciplinary team working on the enquiry into a national disaster). Power is invested in experts in their individual area. The team will have a manager/leader, but they probably exert relatively little day-to-day influence.

Person culture: Think of a constellation of stars. Here the structure only exists to serve the individual stars who get on with it. Think of a group of doctors in a practice, a small management consultancy, lawyer's practice or maybe a group of parish churches that work in a cluster.

The key in any sort of engagement is to try to work out what sort of organisation you are dealing with. If it is a power culture, it doesn't matter what someone's job title is, they need to be close to or at the centre for their decision to count. If you are dealing with a person culture, you might have great influence on one member but there is no guarantee that this means the wider team will adopt your ideas.

Again, we are talking about the organisational *culture* here, regardless of official structure. As always, this tool is about understanding how an organisation really works rather than being judgmental. Reflecting on his own career, a friend of mine observed that the firm at which he trained had been a person culture. University was a role culture (but with aspects of power culture where it was possible to upset the wrong person). His own experience of subsequent church leadership was a task culture, with a strong focus on getting things done. Interestingly, he described his stint as leader of a theological college as 'a power culture where I was the bottleneck leader!'. Handy's approach is about honest evaluation, not condemnation.

Back to scripture

Power culture

Matthew 2:16–18

When Herod realised that he had been outwitted by the Magi, he was furious, and he gave orders to kill all the boys in Bethlehem and its vicinity who were two years old and under, in accordance with the time he had learned from the Magi. Then what was said through the prophet Jeremiah was fulfilled: 'A voice is heard in Ramah, weeping and great mourning, Rachel weeping for her children, and refusing to be comforted, because they are no more.'

Genesis 40:20–23

Now the third day was Pharaoh's birthday, and he gave a feast for all his officials. He lifted up the heads of the chief cupbearer and the chief baker in the presence of his officials: He restored the chief cupbearer to his position, so that he once again put the cup into Pharaoh's hand – but he impaled the chief baker, just as Joseph had said to them in his interpretation. The chief cupbearer, however, did not remember Joseph; he forgot him.

Herod and Pharaoh are two chilling examples of summary justice – or injustice in both cases. All despots and dictators run *power cultures*. There is no need for the normal processes of trial or any observance of law. Of course, once Joseph's ability to interpret dreams is noticed (Gen. 41:14), he must be brought before Pharaoh. This isn't just a quirky detail, it's how power cultures work – you deal with the individual right at the centre, or no one at all.

Role culture

Acts 25:12

After Festus had conferred with his council, he declared: 'You have appealed to Caesar. To Caesar you will go!'

By contrast, the main parts of the Roman Empire are bureaucratic and nearly all bureaucratic organisations are a *role culture*. Layers of power, systems and accountability need to be navigated – there is no quick justice here. It is an interesting point to ponder – does Paul appeal to Caesar deliberately, knowing it will buy him time and ultimately place him at the heart of the unrelenting Roman Empire? Either way, God uses the opportunity, and the rest is history.

Acts 6:1–4

In those days when the number of disciples was increasing, the Hellenistic Jews among them complained against the Hebraic Jews because their widows were being overlooked in the daily distribution of food. So the Twelve gathered all the disciples together and said, 'It would not be right for us to neglect the ministry of the word of God in order to wait on tables. Brothers and sisters, choose seven men from among you who are known to be full of the Spirit and wisdom. We will turn this responsibility over to them and will give our attention to prayer and the ministry of the word.'

We return to this passage from Acts 6 and the famous feeding of the widows – because this apparently small and uninspiring detail marks a significant moment in the growth of the church, taking it from an organic movement to a real organisation. The Grecian Jewish widows are being overlooked so the disciples decide it is someone's 'role' to look after welfare, while it's the disciples' role to preach and teach. A *role culture* is born, and with good reason.

Task culture

Ezra 3:7–11

Then they gave money to the masons and carpenters, and gave food and drink and olive oil to the people of Sidon and Tyre, so that they would bring cedar logs by sea from Lebanon to Joppa, as authorized by Cyrus king of Persia. In the second month of the second year after their arrival at the house of God in Jerusalem, Zerubbabel son of Shealtiel, Joshua son of Jozadak and the rest of the began the work. They appointed Levites twenty years old and older to supervise the building of the house of the Lord. Joshua and his sons and brothers joined together in supervising those working on the house of God. When the builders laid the foundation of the temple of the LORD, the priests in their vestments and with trumpets, and the Levites (the sons of Asaph) with cymbals, took their places to praise the LORD, as prescribed by David king of Israel. With praise and thanksgiving they sang to the LORD: 'He is good; his love toward Israel endures forever.' And all the people gave a great shout of praise to the LORD, because the foundation of the house of the LORD was laid.

Anyone who has ever been involved with a building (or rebuilding) project will be able to understand this story. The details may have changed since two and a half thousand years ago, but the process resonates across time. The temple is to be rebuilt following the period of exile, so tradesmen take it in turns to work. The individuals are specialists, but the organisation pulls them together into a cohesive and productive *task culture*. The passage specifically mentions masons and carpenters, but the Levites are the project managers, and the priests play their role in reminding everyone the real purpose of the task.

Person culture

Acts 15:36–41

Some time later Paul said to Barnabas, 'Let us go back and visit the believers in all the towns where we preached the word of the Lord and see how they are doing.' Barnabas wanted to take John, also called Mark, with them, but Paul did not think it wise to take him, because he had deserted them in Pamphylia and had not continued with them in the work. They had such a sharp disagreement that they parted company. Barnabas took Mark and sailed for Cyprus, but Paul chose Silas and left, commended by the believers to the grace of the Lord. He went through Syria and Cilicia, strengthening the churches.

This is an intriguing little example of *person culture*. As far as we know, there was no specific 'church planting' organisation supervising this process – merely a group of devoted individuals. Although I've also used this passage before as an example of a dispute, the context is fascinating. Both Paul and Barnabas were highly experienced and successful church planters. They could have chosen to continue to work together but didn't. Both were capable and both continued with that calling, albeit on their own or with different companions. It wasn't about the organisation, it was about the people – a great example of a person culture.

And finally…

The Church in the West has been rocked by scandal, time and again, when individuals in Christian leadership have been caught exploiting their position for financial gain, sexual gratification, or the exercise of power. Somewhat remarkable is that in every case, there will have undoubtably been safeguarding policies in place – with trustees or directors supervising them, and to whom they were accountable. In practice, these systems did not work: an excellent example of 'culture eating strategy for breakfast'. This reinforces again the reality that organisational culture may be very different to organisational structure – and why it's vital for those of us in Christian leadership to regularly and honestly assess the culture of our churches.

Another symptom of power culture can be so-called Founder Syndrome, where the founder of an organisation continues to exert a disproportionate amount of power and influence long after things should have moved on; sometimes even from beyond the grave.

A company or charity may find themselves somehow in the grip of a long-dead pioneer, psychologically paralysed by the question, 'What would The Founder do?'

Fans of political theory may have come across Michel's 'Iron law of oligarchy' – the tendency for most organisations, regardless of structure, to tend towards a centralisation of power in the hands of one individual or a small group. For this reason, a number of the examples we will consider here focus on the dangers of power culture in organisations. In the case of charities, I have observed strong leaders who manage to pack their board of trustees (to whom they are accountable) with sympathetic friends and supporters who are unable to challenge them. The tendency to oligarchy was a theme recurrent in the written works of George Orwell, who used it largely as the plot of *Animal Farm* and also alluded to it in *1984*.

It is also important in this context to consider the concept of narcissistic leadership, where a domineering leader's objectives are all about meeting their own needs for recognition and importance. Some level of narcissistic personality can be harnessed into inspiring and courageous leadership, but the danger is when the needs of the leader take over from the needs of the organisation. In stark contrast to this is Jesus' extraordinary briefing for mission in Luke 10, in which He encompasses the possibility of failure: 'When you enter a town and are not welcomed...' (Luke 10:8). Good leaders do not rest their own perception of success and security solely on the fortunes of their organisations. Be alert to the fact that power cultures will often be led by narcissistic leaders.

For many of us, it is a major learning experience to grasp for the first time that the presented structure of an organisation does not represent how it really functions – especially when we're talking about Christian organisations. It can raise feelings of instability and even cynicism. Even our own workplace may be a case in point. Many of us will know the feeling of frustration when some decisions seem to follow a designated process, yet others are taken in a seemingly arbitrary way by a senior leader.

While I'm convinced of the importance of honest evaluation, both positive and negative, I stress again that there is not necessarily any moral judgment attached to any particular organisational culture. Organisations that are support structures for charismatic leaders can be very efficient to deal with. Decisions get made quickly and are, in my experience, fulfilled. Ultimately, the major skill to get into your toolbox is the ability to recognise what is going on, and adjust your approach accordingly.

CHAPTER 11:
FUNCTIONAL LEADERSHIP

It's not what you do, it's the way that you do it... or is it?

There was a chronic tension between his outward appearance, of vigour and openness, and an inner reality of frailty and pain.

Max Hastings on J. F. Kennedy's leadership function in the Cuban missile crisis[1]

The quality of leadership is probably the single most important factor that will determine the success or failure of any given endeavour. So what constitutes leadership quality?

There are lots of different mainstem theories and models of leadership that have been developed over the last few decades, and we'll look at some of them over the next few chapters. Since the mid-1800s, the trait model of leadership has been a pretty dominant one. This is also known more colloquially as the 'great man' theory and broadly supposes that leaders are born, not made. As such, this model proposes that the key task in an organisation is to find one of these natural born leaders – either inside or outside the organisation – and put them in charge. Interestingly, much of the early Christian leadership literature was a variation on this with the 'great' part simply being interpreted as an extended essay on Christian virtue and character. Despite widespread dismissal of the relevance of the trait model, culturally it still has a powerful hold. Many organisations (both corporate and educational) justify very high salaries by asserting the need to get the right person for the role. It may no longer be exclusively a 'great man' that is being sought, but the cultural assumption remains that there is some exceptional individual out there who can be enticed in to transform the fortunes of the organisation.

With a totally different way of looking at this, let me introduce you to John Adair. He had a wide-ranging and varied career encompassing the military; being deckhand on an Icelandic trawler; a stint as a hospital theatre assistant; roles in higher education. I suspect this breadth of experience is a major contributor to the applicability of his thinking! Adair's concept of Functional Leadership (sometimes called Action Centred Leadership) is one of the simplest, most profound, and most important. Adair's insight, first developed in the 1960s, was revolutionary in that instead of focusing on 'traits', Adair focused clinically not on what leaders are *like*, but what they *do*.

Bible stories

John 19:17–18,23–25

Carrying his own cross, [Jesus] went out to the place of the Skull (which in Aramaic is called Golgotha). There they crucified him, and with him two others – one on each side and Jesus in the middle. [...] When the soldiers crucified Jesus, they took his clothes, dividing them into four shares, one for each of them, with the undergarment remaining. This garment was seamless, woven in one piece from top to bottom.

'Let's not tear it,' they said to one another. 'Let's decide by lot who will get it.'

This happened that the scripture might be fulfilled that said, 'They divided my clothes among them and cast lots for my garment.' So this is what the soldiers did. Near the cross of Jesus stood his mother, his mother's sister, Mary the wife of Clopas, and Mary Magdalene.

The passion is, arguably, the central most important act in Jesus' earthly ministry. It is the centrepiece of the faith of a quarter of the earth's population. It is a seminal story, but seldom used to illustrate Jesus' leadership.

Jesus has led His twelve disciples (and a much larger group of individuals associated with His ministry) for three years. Our traditional view of the passion story sees Jesus at His most weak and vulnerable, but the reality is that, despite everything, Jesus is still the leader, still carrying responsibility for His group – and the story is not over yet.

Matthew 8:23–24

Then he got into the boat and his disciples followed him. Suddenly a furious storm came up on the lake, so that the waves swept over the boat. But Jesus was sleeping.

Crisis is the great crucible of leadership. Jeopardy and how we handle it tends to be a blunt indicator of who has initiative and who does not. The disciples are in real danger. What is the best strategy for addressing this and how will it work out?

The theory

Adair's model of leadership is brilliant in that it is fundamentally very simple, but with optional layers of complexity that can be explored once the basics are grasped. Specifically, Adair notes:

- The team has an objective or clearly defined *task* for which it has been created and functions;

- To achieve or complete the task, the *team* needs to function at a high level with each individual fulfilling a specific role, and;

- The team itself is comprised of *individuals* whose needs (including motivation and care) have to be met.

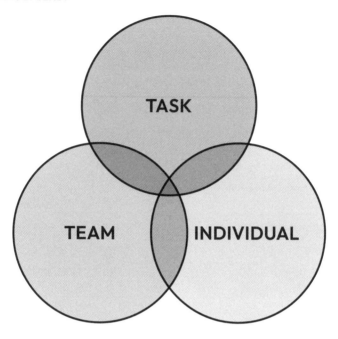

These key terms are worth exploring. Whatever individual work we have, this model is centred on the kind of *task* that can only be achieved by a group working together. Establishing and maintaining the *team* needs to be an intentional and high-priority task for the leader. Great teams don't just happen by accident. Having said that, a good leader also needs to recognise the needs of the *individual* members, which of course may vary from day to day. One individual might be needing motivation, for example, while another needs to be supported to handle a personal crisis. So despite the overall simplicity of the model structure, this overlap is where the complexity comes in.

If you are struggling to visualise this, a cliched but effective illustration is a football team. No striker can win the match: the *task* can only be achieved by the *team*, but each *individual* has a unique and vital role. The defence need to keep opposition goals out, the midfield needs to deliver the ball to the strikers and the strikers need to get it in the back of the net.

Thinking around *task* is often the simplest – after all, it is often what the team has been established for.

Teams need constant maintenance and, as a leader, you may find yourself drawing on several tools to do this such as conflict resolution, or identifying team roles (eg Belbin).

Individual needs will include obvious ones such as salary, but will also encompass much more subtle requirements such as recognition, status, or motivation.

The overlapping of the circles in the diagram is not accidental, and deficiency in any one area will affect the overall performance in a predictable (or sometimes unpredictable) manner! Thanks to its simplicity, this approach is universally applicable from a prayer triplet to a FTSE 100 company.

Adair expands the idea of the leader's role into eight specific tasks (this list is a great example of Do/Manage/Lead as a way of working, with the leader seamlessly transitioning between different needs):

1. *Identifying and clarifying* the task or objective for the team. This may be simple, multiple or complex and may need to be broken down into steps or SMART[2] objectives.

2. Developing a *plan* to achieve the objective or task. At best this may be in consultation with team members drawing on their experience and knowledge, creative and open to different ways of achieving the objective.

3. Teams and specific individuals need to be *briefed*. Communication is key here and this will set the atmosphere and sense of motivation for the team.

4. The leader needs to *manage* the process and *control* the team for maximum impact and best use of resources.

5. Process and achievements need to be *evaluated* both during and at the end of the process. This is a particularly clinical skill requiring objective judgment.

6. *Motivation* is key, both at the start of the process but also as progress unfolds.

7. Team, resources and process all need to be *organised*, particularly in response to unforeseen developments.

8. Team leaders need to *set an example*. Inevitably, poor choices and actions will draw more team attention than good ones. Note that this is the only time Adair strays into the areas of *personality* as a critical factor in leadership.

I want to home in on one very specific point here. Much Christian leadership literature emphasises the *character* of the leader. Of course it's absolutely true that we are called to be honest – people of integrity, courage and compassion – but good character does not automatically make good leadership. Adair's model offers a balancing perspective, focusing not just on leadership traits but primarily on what the leader *does*. This is not only insightful, it's liberating! And here are some reasons why:

- We all tend to be inspired by great leaders we know or have read about. Here is the good news: if Adair is right, you don't have to be *like* them. Be yourself! If you arrange the task, team and individuals in a way that works, you are a good leader.

- Most of us are painfully aware of our own fallings – especially if our hero leader is Jesus, or Saint Paul. Sometimes we feel like fakes. Here is the good news: if you arrange the task, team...

- Sometimes we are just having a bad day, knocked backwards by life events, or hurt by an insensitive comment. Functional leadership does not require us to put on a brave face, (though it may help with motivation and 'setting an example') – just *do* the right things.

- Above all, this model tells us that leaders do not have to be born, they can be 'made' through systematic training.

Given that last point, you won't be surprised to learn that in addition to medicine, the other great practitioner of this leadership model is the military. I once spent considerable time as chaplain ('padre') to a squadron of the Air Cadets. Whilst some youth workers are uncomfortable with the para-military nature of such organisations, I think their immense strength is in quite consciously *teaching leadership*. One young man told me of how he had started working at age 16 in a shoe shop. With pride he declared, 'I should just be working on the shop floor, but because of what I have learned here, I'm now the manager.' Whilst there was some focus on character, I have to say that the approach in the Air Cadets was very much a practical one of functional leadership. It works.

Culturally, functional leadership is a huge challenge to those of us in a church context. Functional leadership does not negate the concept of 'calling' or 'vocation', but challenges us to consider whether those leaders we need are (in some form), already in front of us but needing to be *trained*. In the context of church leadership, it is invariably the character failings that get the headlines – the ones that lead to scandal and disillusion. But what about the many church members frustrated by leaders who are of exemplary character, but simply not particularly good at the leadership function? As I said in the Introduction, King David is commended for he 'shepherded them with integrity of heart; with skilful hands he led them' (Psa. 78:7). Too much Christian literature has emphasised the 'heart' and neglected the 'skill'. Our traditional model of small-church leadership is that of a minister who does everything, and therefore inevitably does some tasks badly. We might define the balancing of these two vital components – heart and skill – as the nucleus of Christian leadership.

Modern critiques of Adair often centre on his relevance in a new age of relatively flat organisational structures. Functional leadership is seen as an authoritarian model from a bygone era, perhaps still relevant in the military but less so in modern, less hierarchical workplaces. Despite that, many other organisations see the three overlapping circles as highly relevant, and action-centred leadership is still widely taught.

Back to scripture

John 19:26–27

When Jesus saw his mother there, and the disciple whom he loved standing nearby, he said to her, 'Woman, here is your son,' and to the disciple, 'Here is your mother.' From that time on, this disciple took her into his home.

As valedictory speeches go, this must be one of the most dramatic in history. Famously there are seven sayings of Jesus from the cross, and here, in the third, Jesus sets up the future care of His mother, Mary, with John. At a human level Jesus is dying in agony, but at a leadership level, He is functionally getting the job done, identifying a task, and allocating an individual within the team.

Matthew 8:23–26

Suddenly a furious storm came up on the lake, so that the waves swept over the boat. But Jesus was sleeping. The disciples went and woke him, saying, 'Lord, save us! We're going to drown!'

He replied, 'You of little faith, why are you so afraid?' Then he got up and rebuked the winds and the waves, and it was completely calm.

This infuriatingly brief account of the storm appears in all three synoptic Gospels and is usually used to illustrate Jesus' lordship over the elements. When I get to heaven, I am going to find out *which* disciple had the wit to wake Jesus. I am sure that they were already furiously bailing water back over the sides of the boat. It is nice to appear calm and serene when in a position of leadership and under pressure – but remember, functional leadership is focused on doing the right thing, not on heroically appearing calm.

And finally...

It is almost taken for granted in western culture that leaders should be a figurehead – the public face of the organisation. With that often comes the assumption that they will be charismatic and engaging speakers, both funny and inspirational. So it's a bit of a surprise that two of our great Bible heroes, Moses and Paul, were both pretty poor speakers. Neither would be invited to do a TED Talk. Moses certainly claims this whilst bargaining with God over leading His people out of slavery (Exod. 4:1). In an easy-to-miss aside, Moses basically says to God, 'I haven't got any better at public speaking since we started this conversation!' – and there is an extended dialogue about Moses' verbal inadequacy, resulting in Aaron being dispatched to be his mouthpiece. Likewise, Paul's oratory skills fall majestically short of our modern expectations – and he certainly doesn't have five bullet points all beginning with the same letter. In 1 Corinthians 10:10, Paul acknowledges that some consider him 'unimpressive'. Later, he develops this idea that he is not in the same league as the gifted super-apostles: 'But I do not think I am in the least inferior... I may not be a trained speaker, but I do have knowledge' (1 Cor. 11:6). And if Paul's not a super-apostle, who is?! His results speak for themselves and should be a powerful antidote to our dominant preoccupation with leadership style.

A friend of mine worked for years at a major NHS hospital as a consultant on the crash team – they're nothing to do with Accident and Emergency, but the team that comes running in if your heart stops on a ward. Summoned by a pager, they would congregate around the patient and the first question asked was, 'Who is leading today?' One of the team would immediately identify themselves and swiftly commence with the business of resuscitation: adrenalin, CPR, defibrillation etc. The next day, the same patient could arrest again. The same team assemble, but this time it's a different doctor calling the shots. So, what do we learn here? This is an unusual but not unique situation. All the medical staff were very experienced and hugely talented. Any one of the doctors *could* lead the team, but the leadership role was rotated between them, taking it in turns. There might be several possible medical interventions, or combinations of interventions, but mattered was that first, someone *made some decisions* and secondly, they made decisions *quickly*. The team might well meet on other occasions and discuss the broad approach to patient care but, in the moment, the need to address the three key areas of task, team and individual was very acute – literally a matter of life and death.

Critics of Adair might push back quite strongly here. When we look at transformational leadership in chapter 13, we will see that appearing calm in a crisis (rather than just getting stuff done) might turn out to be not only helpful, but inspiring. The same critics might note that *how* we do things might matter as much as *what* we do. The end cannot justify the means if it is cruel or unhelpful to either the leader or the led.

In many respects, our modern cultural awareness of the importance of leadership is commendable but it has resulted in a bewildering variety of theories, literature, and sometimes contradictory recommendations. Functional leadership is a great place to start the leadership journey. The simplicity of Adair's thinking sweeps through like a breath of fresh air. As numerous musicians have sung: 'It ain't what you do, it's the way that you do it' – an enduring lyric. It's a great song, but 100% wrong. When it comes to leadership, it's not how we do it, it's *what we do*, says Adair, that matters.

CHAPTER 12:
SITUATIONAL LEADERSHIP

It all depends... but on what?

A person is no simple one-dimensional self. Here is a labyrinth within the soul. What we think and desire often comes into conflict with what we do.

John O'Donohue[1]

Leading God-created human beings is hard! The aim of the tools in this book is to make this hugely challenging task simpler, to give us abstract understandings of how people think and work, so that we can lead them in effective and rewarding teams. At its heart, however, we know that no model of leadership can encompass the true complexity of human experience. Situational Leadership is powerful for trying to combine simplicity of approach with an acknowledgement that humans and situations are infinitely variable.

As director of a local Christian schools' work charity, I would frequently find myself sitting down with some impressive and high-flying professionals. Headteachers were a good example (£100k starting salary, 150 staff, £6m annual budget), but there were also heads of local charities, social service departments and even businesspeople who funded us, and more than one retired military person on the board of trustees. Many of them had a lot of professional leadership training or were exercising leadership in their roles, and I found it vital to be able to dialogue with them on leadership issues. Situational Leadership is a concept that you may well come across, even though (in my experience) it is less likely to be talked about than some of the other models we are examining. Despite this, it is a significant theory in the arsenal of leadership thinking.

Paul Hersey and Kenneth Blanchard worked together on this approach in 1982. Whilst John Adair focused on what a leader *does*, Hersey and Blanchard considered the question: how does what you do *change* with a changing situation or team? What do you need to bring to the leadership table as contexts develop and vary? Situational Leadership posits that what is needed is not one over-arching leadership style, but the ability to respond and change as a situation demands.

First, let's consider Contingency Theory, the thinking that Hersey and Blanchard were without a doubt building on. Since the 1950s, leadership experts at both Ohio and Chicago universities had been exploring the idea that there was not one best way of leading, but that skilled leaders might need to adapt their leadership style to circumstances – so leadership is contingent on a specific situation. Fred Fiedler developed this more in the 1990s, explaining that most leaders were somewhere on a continuum between task orientation (just get the job done) and relationship orientation (keep the team happy). Fiedler developed some simple analytical tools for this but basically gave us a simple, two-dimensional model. If we are aware of our own style, and the specific challenges of our situation, then armed with this insight we can adapt our leadership (more or less task/relationship orientation) according to circumstances. Hersey and Blanchard's model is a more sophisticated development of this thinking.

Bible stories

Luke 7:1–3a

When Jesus had finished saying all this to the people who were listening, he entered Capernaum. There a centurion's servant, whom his master valued highly, was sick and about to die. The centurion heard of Jesus and sent some elders of the Jews to him, asking him to come.

Like so many Bible narratives, the economy of description in this account hides a mass of conflicting and complex cultural issues. Jesus' ministry at this point seems to have been that of an itinerant rabbi. He had a close team of disciples and a wider group of friends and supporters. As a member of the occupying Roman forces, the centurion would be hated and despised, but tolerated. His servant may have been Roman but equally possibly someone employed locally. If the latter, this alone would have given him an ambiguous status in the local community, although his actual employment status would be closer to that of a slave. It is astonishing that the elders ask Jesus to intervene on behalf of a Gentile. What is going on?

2 Kings 5:1–3

Now Naaman was commander of the army of the king of Aram. He was a great man in the sight of his master and highly regarded, because through him the LORD had given victory to Aram. He was a valiant soldier, but he had leprosy.

Now bands of raiders from Aram had gone out and had taken captive a young girl from Israel, and she served Naaman's wife. She said to her mistress, 'If only my master would see the prophet who is in Samaria! He would cure him of his leprosy.'

There are some fascinating commonalities and differences between these two passages. This time it is the master that is ill and the servant that is the agent in the story. In this case the slave girl's fortunes are tied up with Naaman's but at an emotional level, she has little reason to wish him well. Her status really is the lowest in the household and it is a fragile sequence of connections that gets Naaman to even consider seeing Elisha. Circumstantial evidence indicates that Naaman has little or no idea who he was, and perhaps it is desperation that drives what follows.

The theory

Hersey and Blanchard's theory comes in three linked parts, so let's break it down.

First, we have four leadership styles:

- Telling: this is pretty directive – as leader, I tell you what to do and how.

- Selling: this is more dialogical as I persuade and motivate you with my vision.

- Participating: this is less directive and I allow you to contribute ideas and energy.

- Delegating: this is truly 'hands off' – I let you take responsibility and get on with it.

Secondly, as a good leader I need to be able to assess both the ability and motivation levels of my team members. Situational leadership gives us a four-part matrix:

- M1: Group members lack the knowledge, skills, and willingness to complete the task.

- M2: Group members are willing and enthusiastic but lack the ability.

- M3: Group members have the skills and capability to complete the task but are unwilling to take responsibility.

- M4: Group members are highly skilled and willing to complete the task.

Thirdly, as leaders we *match* our leadership style to the individual:

- Low maturity (M1)—Telling

- Medium maturity (M2)—Selling

- Medium maturity (M3)—Participating

- High maturity (M4)—Delegating

Hersey and Blanchard suggest we consider four key elements in implementing this theory:

1: Consider the relationship. A newly formed or unsure team might need a much more authoritarian style of leadership to give a sense of safety and competence. A well-established, proven team would probably resent this and needs a more democratic style with significant delegation of authority. So, we are likely to find ourselves using a lot more M1 and M2 with a new team, more M3 and M4 with a well-established team.

2: Consider the task. Is it simple or complex? How is it measured? Can we really 'evangelise Birmingham', become 'market leader in our field' or 'eradicate cancer' – and how do we know when the task is complete, or the target achieved?

3: Consider the level of authority of the leader. Paid staff may or may not be highly motivated but depending on our leadership context, we may find we are dealing with those who are disillusioned and demotivated. Pay is no guarantee of motivation, indeed, volunteers (by definition) often have strong ideological reasons for being on our teams. The lesson here is to analyse each situation rather than assuming any particular level of motivation. Some staff may have complex personal reasons for being there. Our leadership style must acknowledge this, or we can lose people. Again, we need to consider which style of leadership is most appropriate, even down to each individual.

4: Consider the level of maturity of the individual. This is always key and, as noted above, it can change! By definition, M1 and M2 are more directive but also more supportive styles of leadership. We might have a team member who is going through a difficulty, and it might well be appropriate to, say, revert to an M2 style even though they have been at M3 previously.

Like all great theories, situational leadership is fundamentally simple but still takes time to implement skilfully. It allows us to lead in different ways with different people but also requires the skill of constantly re-analysing and updating our understanding. People and situations change over time. Imagine you are supervising an intern or new recruit. We would expect them to start as M2 (high motivation/low skill), but with setbacks there is always the danger of slipping into M1. With training and an apprenticeship-style programme we would, however, expect them to progress to M3 and ultimately be able to safely give them significant responsibility (M4). Our skill as leaders is to get the timing and expectation right!

Back to scripture

Luke 7:3–9

The centurion heard of Jesus and sent some elders of the Jews to him, asking him to come and heal his servant. When they came to Jesus, they pleaded earnestly with him, 'This man deserves to have you do this, because he loves our nation and has built our synagogue.' So Jesus went with them.

He was not far from the house when the centurion sent friends to say to him: 'Lord, don't trouble yourself, for I do not deserve to have you come under my roof. That is why I did not even consider myself worthy to come to you. But say the word, and my servant will be healed. For I myself am a man under authority, with soldiers under me. I tell this one, "Go," and he goes; and that one, "Come," and he comes. I say to my servant, "Do this," and he does it.'

When Jesus heard this, he was amazed at him, and turning to the crowd following him, he said, 'I tell you, I have not found such great faith even in Israel.'

Many of us will be familiar with this story. The soldier's servant is gravely ill and, as an outsider, he skilfully delegates the request for healing to local leaders who are both confident and motivated (M4). Interestingly, the local elders are concerned that whilst Jesus has the ability, he may not have the motivation to heal a member of the resented Roman occupying force – they think Jesus may be M3. Jesus of course heals the servant and prompts an observation from the centurion that His normal leadership style is 'telling' – He has no need to persuade anyone to follow His instructions!

2 Kings 5:4,6–11,13–16,19

So Naaman left, taking with him ten talents of silver, six thousand shekels of gold and ten sets of clothing. [...] The letter that he took to the king of Israel read: 'With this letter I am sending my servant Naaman to you so that you may cure him of his leprosy.'

As soon as the king of Israel read the letter, he tore his robes and said, 'Am I God? Can I kill and bring back to life? See how he is trying to pick a quarrel with me!'

Elisha sent him this message: 'Have the man come to me and he will know that there is a prophet in Israel.' So Naaman stopped at the door of Elisha's house. Elisha sent a messenger to say to him, 'Go, wash yourself seven times in the Jordan, and your flesh will be restored and you will be cleansed.'

But Naaman went away angry and said, 'I thought that he would surely come out to me and stand and call on the name of the LORD his God, wave his hand over the spot and cure me of my leprosy...' [...] Naaman's servants said, 'My father, if the prophet had told you to do some great thing, would you not have done it? How much more, then, when he tells you, "Wash and be cleansed"!' So he went down and dipped himself in the Jordan seven times, as the man of God had told him, and his flesh was restored and became clean like that of a young boy.

Then Naaman went back to the man of God and said, 'Now I know that there is no God in all the world except in Israel. So please accept a gift from your servant.'

The prophet answered, 'As surely as the LORD lives, whom I serve, I will not accept a thing.' And even though Naaman urged him, he refused. [...] 'Go in peace,' Elisha said.

The captured Israelite slave girl recommends the prophet Elisha's healing gift to her master. As Naaman is held in high regard by his king, the monarch sponsors the trip but to the wrong man, assuming that only a rival king would have the ability and motivation (M4). Finally, he is directed to Elisha (whom he might initially have assumed to be lacking in ether ability or motivation – M1). Naaman however is insulted by the simple directive to wash in the Jordan (Elisha chooses a 'telling' style of leadership); the task seems too easy, or perhaps Naaman wanted to be consulted and discuss the requirements for healing with Elisha (he expects a 'selling' or 'participative' leadership style from the prophet). In later verses, Elisha's corrupt servant decides to pick up on this and exploit Naaman's expectation that the task should be more costly, a course of action that ultimately rebounds on him with disastrous consequences.

John 15:15–17

I no longer call you servants, because a servant does not know his master's business. Instead, I have called you friends, for everything that I learned from my Father I have made known to you. You did not choose me, but I chose you and appointed you so that you might go and bear fruit – fruit that will last – and so that whatever you ask in my name the Father will give you. This is my command: Love each other.

I love this quite astonishing passage. Jesus has every right to simply tell us what to do (telling). But that would be the relationship of a servant, not a friend. Instead, He shares His vison and calling and involves the disciples in it – the leadership style is participative, and following His death, resurrection and the coming of the Holy Spirit, it will become truly delegated.

Ecclesiastes 8:2–4

Obey the king's command, I say, because you took an oath before God. Do not be in a hurry to leave the king's presence. Do not stand up for a bad cause, for he will do whatever he pleases. Since a king's word is supreme, who can say to him, 'What are you doing?'

Leaders don't always get it right. This short passage really is a condemnation of the 'telling' style of leadership – if that is the *only* style you have. In the context of this passage from Ecclesiastes, it is clear that the author recognises that leaders often do get it wrong, and teams need to be able to challenge this – which is an integral feature of a participative or delegatory style of leadership.

Genesis 41:33–41

'And now let Pharaoh look for a discerning and wise man and put him in charge of the land of Egypt. Let Pharaoh appoint commissioners over the land to take a fifth of the harvest of Egypt during the seven years of abundance. They should collect all the food of these good years that are coming and store up the grain under the authority of Pharaoh, to be kept in the cities for food. This food should be held in reserve for the country, to be used during the seven years of famine that will come upon Egypt, so that the country may not be ruined by the famine.'

The plan seemed good to Pharaoh and to all his officials. So Pharaoh asked them, 'Can we find anyone like this man, one in whom is the spirit of God?'

Then Pharaoh said to Joseph, 'Since God has made all this known to you, there is no one so discerning and wise as you. You shall be in charge of my palace, and all my people are to submit to your orders. Only with respect to the throne will I be greater than you.'

So Pharaoh said to Joseph, 'I hereby put you in charge of the whole land of Egypt.'

Joseph's rise out of imprisonment is meteoric. We could challenge Pharaoh's assumption that dream interpretation qualified someone to be national economic advisor, but note that there is a logic – Joseph's appointment is predicated on the recognition that Joseph has the Holy Spirit in abundance (see verse 38 and, in the spirit of Psalm 1, 'all he does prospers'). Either way, it is a delegating leadership style responding to recognition of an M4 person of ability and motivation.

And finally…

When I took over a schools' work organisation, I inherited the team that was in existence. We had a large team of volunteers as well as several salaried posts. Thankfully I didn't have anyone who fell into the M1 category, but I did have a capable but somewhat unmotivated M3 who I had to inspire with a 'participative' leadership style. I also had a much more enthusiastic worker who had some energy, but they were younger and lacked both skill and experience (M2). A mixture of 'telling' and 'selling' style made the most of his energy and enthusiasm and helped him gain the skills he needed. Fortunately, I also inherited a brilliant and motivated administrator who, if I'm honest, pretty much ran the organisation at the beginning of my tenure (M4). She knew what needed doing and when, and kept me on the straight and narrow. I was free to lead the big-picture stuff whilst she managed much of the organisation on a day-to-day basis. She responded well to a completely delegated style and thrived on the trust I put in her.

   Leadership can be enormously complex and nuanced. Adapting my leadership style to the individuals took a huge amount of time and effort. The frank reality was that I might not have chosen to employ some of them if I had stated from scratch, but I had inherited them because they were already employed. Understanding their individual needs took much time and patience, including many conversations in car journeys between schools. This was vital, however, if I was to really bring out the best in all the individuals. Whilst we were a relatively small team, we were also a highly disparate one. Even the volunteers had a real range of overlapping reasons for being part of the team. I have always argued that managing organisations with both paid and volunteer staff is one of the most complex leadership contexts possible. It was a challenging time but also a deeply satisfying one. Situational leadership may seem a complex model but may also be the key to unlocking your world.

CHAPTER 13: TRANSFORMATIONAL LEADERSHIP

Taking it to the next level

We shall fight on the beaches, we shall fight on the landing grounds, we shall fight in the fields and in the streets, we shall fight in the hills; we shall never surrender...

Winston Churchill, June 1940

For those of us who regularly speak in public, Winston Churchill's speeches are the stuff of dreams. Legend has it that after delivering this wartime monologue in 1940, Churchill sat down amid rapturous applause, turned to a colleague, and said quietly, 'We will fight them with the butt end of broken bottles, because that's bloody well all we've got.'[1] For me this additional detail adds to his appeal. Churchill was not being dishonest. He knew the odds, but also understood that what people needed at that moment was not a sober analysis of the chances of defeat but the chance to believe in the possibility of victory. And while Churchill was one of the obvious greats, transformational leaders may well be charismatic in style and personality, but it's not an essential requirement. This approach is about working in a particular way, not style.

Transformational leaders are good because they manage to convey a compelling vision of the importance of what an organisation is doing. Modern capitalism is great at meeting most of humanity's basic needs. Frequently however, employment in these organisations leaves us far from any sense of purpose or meaningful achievement. There is a very old story of a man who goes up to two workers labouring beside each other and asks them, 'What are you doing?' The first replies, 'Well, we're making this stone wall.' The other says, 'Can't you see? I'm building a cathedral.' The latter works for a transformational leader.

My adult son once gave this devastating indictment of a local church leader we both knew: 'He's a lovely guy... but you wouldn't follow him into battle!' As a leader I don't just want to get stuff done (functional leadership); I don't just want to clinically adjust my style to maximise the output of my team (situational leadership); I want to see people inspired, for the kingdom of God, and even running ahead of where I am.

James MacGregor Burns introduced the concept of Transformational Leadership in 1978 and defined it as 'a process where leaders and their followers raise one another to higher levels of morality and motivation'.[2] I find this intriguing: whilst not specifically Christian in concept, I can easily see why this model resonates in a faith context. I have observed over many years that for many of us who attend church or go to big Christian events, there can be a taken for granted feeling about inspirational speaking and leadership. You may, like me, have had that experience of switching into preaching mode whilst presenting in a secular context (maybe a sales meeting or on an educational programme) and been surprised at the emotional impact of what you are doing. This is a taste of transformational leadership.

Bible stories

John 13:1

It was just before the Passover Festival. Jesus knew that the hour had come for him to leave this world and go to the Father. Having loved his own who were in the world, he now showed them the full extent of his love.

Translating the end this verse is tricky. Some editions translate it as 'he loved them to the end'. Either way, John 13 marks the start of an extraordinary discourse. What's love got to do with... leadership? Well, love actually turns out to have a huge amount to do with it. We will use this chapter (as well as verses from the story of David, the flawed but passionate Old Testament leader) to explore this a bit further.

The theory

MacGregor Burns may have founded the concept of transformational leadership but, like all great ideas, he stood on the shoulders of giants. In this case it was Bernard M. Bass, an academic scholar, who first brought a slightly more rigorous, analytic and clinical level of thinking, emphasising the need to not just inspire but to get concrete results (whereas I would acknowledge MacGregor Burns as being more revolutionary with emphasis on the aspects of moral and emotional leadership). According to Bass, transformational leaders:

- Set clear goals with high expectations;

- Are encouragers;

- Provide support and recognition;

- Stir emotion;

- Inspire people to look beyond their self-interest;

- Inspire people to reach for the improbable.

Again, the resonance with Christian ministry and leadership values is clear. Transformational leadership is also unusual in putting emotional factors, such as inspiration, central to its way. This is in stark contrast to so many leadership theories that tend towards a dispassionate, scientific approach. Before we get carried away with this grand vision for leadership, it's worth reminding ourselves that the reality rests on hard thinking and hard work. So, drawing on mainstream thinking, here is the recipe for becoming a Transformational Leader:

Step 1: Create an inspiring vision. People need a reason to be a follower and be on your team. Is it clear what your organisation is doing and how it will achieve its goal? I have spent much of my career leading teams working with young people. To be honest, I suspect many folks were on my team because it was clear we were serving young people, giving them chances to become and grow as disciples. What we did as a team worked, so the team members bought into that vision and success.

Step 2: Motivate people to buy into and deliver the vision. This is a whole subject in itself and, for a recap, you can revisit Kotter's eight-step process of change. To summarise: start small but with a clear idea; work to gain some quick wins; celebrate those; grow from them and anchor this in the culture of the organisation. Saying to someone, 'I'm thinking of doing a town-wide mission in two years' time – could you help?' is not inspiring – it's too vague and far off. Saying, 'I'm going into the local school next week – can you help me with an assembly and lunchtime club?' is immediate and clear. Guess which one is likely to elicit a 'Yes!'. Using the SMART acronym is not essential here but helps in ensuring what we offer as leaders is grounded in the short to medium term, and realistic as well as visionary.

Step 3: Manage the delivery of the vision. This may be hard work! This is the humdrum part of just getting on with doing the work, building relationships, praying, and seeing what God does. Remember that unlike functional leadership, transformational leadership is built around you and your personality. Integrity and reliability are more important than charisma and personality. This is a pressure and requires you to be honest, upbeat, and realistic – it's a tough call, but that is why it works. Communication is key for keeping not only your team but also your sponsors (your employer, church, charity, directors, trustees, or backers) in the loop.

I think this stage is one of the most challenging aspects of transformational leadership. It is relatively easy for charismatically gifted presenters to inspire a vison; many then fail to deliver the structures and process. Other leaders may be good at the nuts and bolts but find the ability to inspire others hard. It is a rare combination of gifts to be able to do both aspects well. No personality style disqualifies you from transformational leadership, but it is essential to be able to realistically appraise your own strengths and weaknesses to make this leadership style work effectively in your context. Self-awareness is key!

Remember that once people have bought into the vision, the danger of under-challenging them is just as likely as expecting too much. Warren Buffett notes this with a counter-intuitive and paradoxical insight: 'People don't trust you if you ask them to do stuff that's too easy; ask them to do more difficult things and you'll increase your chances.'[3]

Step 4: Build ever stronger, trust-based relationships. I'm going to be honest: if you get steps 1–3 right, this is the easy bit. People love being on successful teams. People get a huge buzz from really being part of something successful. This is the goal, but enjoy the process and don't take anything for granted. Incidentally, just to finish on a warning, this is why people find it so devastating when leaders fail or fall into temptation. With transformational leadership, people are invested at every level with their time, emotion, and belief, and that is a big responsibility to carry.

Back to scripture

The concluding chapters of John's Gospel contain lots of examples of aspects of transformational leadership, so we will start with some of these and in each case link scripture to the specific tasks of this model:

John 13:2–14

The evening meal was in progress, Jesus knew that the Father had put all things under his power, and that he had come from God and was returning to God; so he got up from the meal, took off his outer clothing, and wrapped a towel round his waist. After that, he poured water into a basin and began to wash his disciples' feet, drying them with the towel that was wrapped round him.

He came to Simon Peter, who said to him, 'Lord, are you going to wash my feet?'

Jesus replied, 'You do not realise now what I am doing, but later you will understand.'

'No,' said Peter, 'you shall never wash my feet.'

Jesus answered, 'Unless I wash you, you have no part with me.'

'Then, Lord,' Simon Peter replied, 'not just my feet but my hands and my head as well!'

Jesus answered, 'Those who have had a bath need only to wash their feet; their whole body is clean. And you are clean, though not every one of you.' For he knew who was going to betray him, and that was why he said not every one was clean.

When he had finished washing their feet, he put on his clothes and returned to his place. 'Do you understand what I have done for you?' he asked them. 'You call me "Teacher" and "Lord", and rightly so, for that is what I am. Now that I, your Lord and Teacher, have washed your feet, you also should wash one another's feet.'

After washing the disciples' feet, Jesus specifically says He has set an *example*. In taking on the role of a servant, Jesus sets a goal, encourages His team, and inspires them to look beyond their self-interest all in one go. Some years ago, my parish did a traditional, mission week. After the final event, the crowds dispersed and at 11pm I found myself and the vicar, David, alone in the hall stacking chairs. 'Look at us,' I quipped, 'You are off to be Bishop of Bradford in a few weeks and I am off to a great job in the diocese, and here we are stacking chairs!' Without a moment's hesitation David replied, 'Nigel, that's servant leadership!'

John 14:12

Very truly I tell you, whoever believes in me will do the works I have been doing, and they will do even greater things than these, because I am going to the Father.

Yes, even greater things. Wow! Jesus asks us to reach for the improbable. I love that this is not just an abstract statement. There is a hint here that 'going to the Father' is a strategic step on the way to Pentecost and the new empowering of the Spirit. *That* is why we will be able to do greater things.

John 15:5

I am the vine; you are the branches. If you remain in me and I in you, you will bear much fruit; apart from me you can do nothing.

Jesus is central to the vision. Note that this is a much more powerful and intimate picture than most of us realise. A vine is *mostly* branches. We are not somehow grafted on to the stem – we are a big, integral part of the plant – and a vital part of the plan! You might say we *are* the plan. This is support *and* recognition.

John 15:15

I no longer call you servants, because a servant does not know his master's business. Instead, I have called you friends, for everything that I learned from my Father I have made known to you.

These are breath-taking and stirring words. Jesus does not follow the 'do what I say' model of leadership: inasmuch as they can understand it, Jesus' disciples have the plan, the vision – nothing is hidden or held back.

Our other source of inspiration is King David, someone whose triumphs and failures as a leader are documented in great detail:

2 Samuel 9:3,5–10

The king asked, 'Is there no one still alive from the house of Saul to whom I can show God's kindness?' Ziba answered the king, 'There is still a son of Jonathan; he is lame in both feet.' So King David had him brought from Lo Debar. When Mephibosheth came to David, he bowed down to pay him honour. David said, 'Mephibosheth!'

'At your service,' he replied. 'Don't be afraid,' David said to him, 'for I will surely show you kindness for the sake of your father Jonathan. I will restore to you all the land that belonged to your grandfather Saul, and you will always eat at my table.'

Mephibosheth said, 'What is your servant, that you should notice a dead dog like me?'

Then the king summoned Ziba, Saul's steward, and said to him, 'I have given your master's grandson everything that belonged to Saul and his family. You and your sons and your servants are to farm the land for him and bring in the crops, so that your master's grandson may be provided for. And Mephibosheth, grandson of your master, will always eat at my table.' (Now Ziba had fifteen sons and twenty servants.)

This is a great story. For the sake of David's long-term friendship with Saul's son Jonathan, he looks up Jonathan's disabled son Mephibosheth and elevates him from the poverty of a beggar's life to live in his royal court. What has this to do with being a great leader? The short answer is, nothing – and that is the whole point. David does not do this because it leads to some military victory or political gain. It is an act of pure altruism and integrity. His starting point is a desire to show kindness. It is not based on any sense of profit or achievement. It is an action inspired by values and the desire to build a kingdom of justice. Ironically, people will notice if you do things like this. Here we are nearly three thousand years later still talking about it.

2 Samuel 23:13–17

During harvest time, three of the thirty chief warriors came down to David at the cave of Adullam, while a band of Philistines was encamped in the Valley of Rephaim. At that time David was in the stronghold, and the Philistine garrison was at Bethlehem. David longed for water and said, 'Oh, that someone would get me a drink of water from the well near the gate of Bethlehem!' So the three mighty warriors broke through the Philistine lines, drew water from the well near the gate of Bethlehem and carried it back to David. But he refused to drink it; instead, he poured it out before the LORD. 'Far be it from me, LORD, to do this!' he said. 'Is it not the blood of men who went at the risk of their lives?' And David would not drink it. Such were the exploits of the three mighty warriors.

This is a quirky and intriguing passage. It doesn't make sense until you remind yourself of the Old Testament sacrificial system – that the first and the best of anything would be sacrificed to God as an offering of worship. Despite coming at the end of 2 Samuel, theologians believe this event probably happened early in David's 'career', when he fled from Saul and was beginning to draw a team or warriors around him. A casual remark regarding his thirst inspires three of them to break through enemy lines, raid a well and bring water back to David. David is so inspired by their loyalty (risking their lives to slake his thirst) that he can't drink the water and instead pours it out as an offering to God (remember the value of water in a desert culture!). He has already inspired people to reach for the improbable and go beyond their own self-interest. Whilst it may read strangely to us, what he does is a significant recognition of the worth of their efforts and risk.

And finally...

A recurring theme in this chapter has been the balance and connection between character and competence that lies within us as leaders. Transformational leadership is embedded within and built on our own character and values. It does, however, also require us to have or develop the abilities to communicate, share, inspire and encourage. Transformational leadership is powerful and potentially dangerous because it really does invite commitment from the whole person, not just the buying of their labour or time. This places huge responsibility with us as leaders. The great theologian Dietrich Bonhoeffer famously said, 'When Christ calls a man, he bids him come and die.'[4] We may be inviting the people we're leading to 'die for something' in the sense that they offer their lives to God for His purposes, but are we asking the right people, in the right way and for the right reason?

During the Falklands War, a British Army officer named Robert Lawrence found himself in the thick of the battle for Mount Tumbledown, a vital piece of high ground. In his book, *When the Fighting is Over*,[5] he describes the moment when, in a move more reminiscent of the First World War, he shouted 'Charge!' and started running across exposed ground at an Argentinian machine gun position. In the moment, he truly had no idea if his men would run with him – but as he glanced right and left, the whole platoon were running together. He graphically describes this as the high point of his life: elating, intoxicating and deeply satisfying. He was later badly injured, rehabilitated, awarded the Military Cross, and had to rebuild both his body and his life. Few of us can read of his exploits without a pang of a strange kind of envy. To see people sold out for a cause that is under your inspiring leadership must truly be a major highlight of a person's life or career. The personal cost may be high, but the rewards can be higher still.

CHAPTER 14:
JUMPING THE CURVE

I make no claim to be a philosopher, but this much I have observed: that when a thing seems at its zenith, you may be sure its destruction has already started.

Tiro, scribe to Cicero in Robert Harris' *Dictator*[1]

This tool is not about day-to-day management or leadership. It's not one that you would ever use at a micro level. This is one to keep in your back pocket for those deep discussions about the future direction of your company, charity, school, project, church, or ministry – perhaps in the run up to an appraisal, an AGM, or a strategy planning day. This tool is all about big picture strategy and direction. Visionaries, this is one for you.

This is another brilliant approach by the great Charles Handy, whose thesis is simply this: the time when things are going well may in fact be your time of greatest danger, because it is then, in the 'good times', that you need to be thinking ahead to the next big adventure.

Bible stories

Acts 10:1–7

At Caesarea there was a man named Cornelius, a centurion in what was known as the Italian Regiment. He and all his family were devout and God-fearing; he gave generously to those in need and prayed to God regularly. One day at about three in the afternoon he had a vision. He distinctly saw an angel of God, who came to him and said, 'Cornelius!'

> Cornelius stared at him in fear. 'What is it, Lord?' he asked.
>
> The angel answered, 'Your prayers and gifts to the poor have come up as a memorial offering before God. Now send men to Joppa to bring back a man named Simon who is called Peter. He is staying with Simon the tanner, whose house is by the sea.'
>
> When the angel who spoke to him had gone, Cornelius called two of his servants and a devout soldier who was one of his attendants.

They say history is written by the victors – at the very least it often excludes any alternative outcomes from our imagination. How might the early history of the Church have turned out differently? This passage shows us a crucial turning point. Like several 'good' centurions, Cornelius seeks a follower of Jesus and invites him to Caesarea. How will Peter respond? History hangs in the balance.

The theory

Handy's observation is that nearly all organisations or 'products' go through a predictable life cycle of a slow start (many commercial enterprises lose money before they start making it), big growth, a levelling off in performance, followed by inevitable decline. Think about football teams; boy bands; the popularity of social media sites (who remembers MySpace and Friends Reunited?!); The British Empire; buying CDs in actual music shops; Formula 1 teams... I could go on. Now, there may be exceptions to this, but we are about to examine how some organisations seem to sustain growth and buck the curve. The solution to beating the apparent inevitability of this lifecycle lies in managing change, courage, and timing. The 'product life-cycle curve' (or theory), had been observed and promoted by Raymond Vernon in 1966, but Handy's insight was to superimpose multiple curves on the original theory.

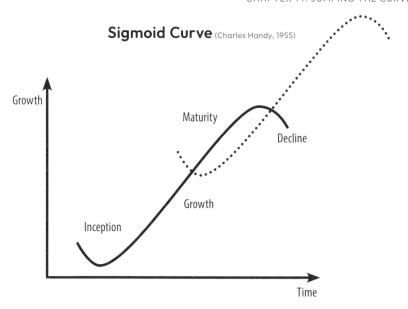

Sigmoid Curve (Charles Handy, 1955)

According to this strategy, if you can anticipate that you are approaching the peak and inevitable decline of your project, you can make changes, instigate a new curve (the dotted one as shown), and begin a new upward trajectory. Fundamentally, it is as simple as that – but this tool needs to come with several health warnings.

First, we have no problem intellectually assenting to the wisdom offered by this tool, which makes it very powerful. The trickier part is applying it to real life. For a start, management diagrams invariably mark the left-hand axis as 'performance' or 'growth'. How do we measure this in actuality? Not all groups or teams deliver quantifiable results. Depending on what organisation you lead, it might be sales revenue, profit, attendance, achievement of your students… what is the correct measure of success that you might insert here? Is it about individuals, growth, just plain numbers, or a combination? And then, how do you measure it? For some organisations there will be a simple answer; for others it may be extremely difficult. For this reason, even the shape of the curve is contentious. If you measure profit, the new curve may indeed dip as the cost of the new project bites into revenue. If it is sales alone, it will start with a flat line – you cannot have negative sales! As with most great theories, we will need to 'adopt and adapt'.

Secondly, diagrams for this model invariably present beautifully smooth curves that grow, level off and decline – that is after all, the whole point of the model. Most organisations will have a much bumpier ride. Growth may not be smooth but instead be marked by spurts of growth followed by small declines, then growth again. This presents a significant challenge. If 'success' (say, attendance at your events) has declined, is that a blip that might be reversed the following year by growth, or a trend – the point at which the organisation is entering a period of sustained decline?

I once worked for a small, independent theological college. Students were our life blood (put simply, their fees paid for the organisation), and we watched enrolment figures like a hawk. Some years, the figures really did dip – and it would have been easy to panic and make big strategic changes to what we were offering too early. Equally, it would have been easy to dismiss the falling-off and plough on. In practice we did develop new growth opportunities (including a master's degree). Trying to interpret what the figures meant was a major task for the leadership group.

Actor and comedian Tim Allen once quipped, 'If it ain't broke, you can probably still fix it.'[2] Making a change when all seems to be going well is counterintuitive. For this reason, it takes incredible courage, wisdom and insight to recognise when the first growth curve, however we measure it, is starting to level off. When that happens, we really do need to take note as the only way from there is down – and it takes much, much longer to turn an organisation around when it has already started to decline. Act too early and you lose the fruits of growth; too late and you are losing already. As a personal observation, having worked with many organisations, I have noticed that once the decline has started, the range of options to turn things around will decline as well. For example, a major rebranding and marketing launch requires funding. Once funds have started to decrease, you may no longer be able to afford this, so that option is no longer on the table. Similarly, new projects require good staff. Once an organisation enters the decline phase, good staff may well leave what is perceived as a sinking ship. Whether they are recognised as such or not, for many organisations, staff are the key asset.

Once they have left, other exciting options will leave with them.

Finally, observe also that if change does bring negative growth in the short run (such as if profits dip before going up), all those resistant to change will be saying, 'We told you so!' Anyone who has worked on a lively board of trustees or company directors will know how scary the process of advocating for change can be. Not for nothing did Kotter make a living from exploring in depth just how to navigate these dangerous waters! The sigmoid curve needs to be handled very carefully; it is not an excuse for change, but it is a brilliant way for a visionary leader to help show their team why they need to embrace change for the future of their work.

Incidentally, a key practical insight to help manage the approach to potential change is to ask yourself as an organisation not, 'What do we do?' but, 'What are we trying to achieve; what service do we offer?' A good example might be this: rather than saying, 'We do a residential with the youth group every year', why not say, 'We want to take young people out of their comfort zone and give them a new opportunity to encounter God in a new way'? The underlying aim stays the same, but the insight allows for change and a new process.

Back to scripture

Acts 10: 9,11–14,19–20,23–24,30–34,44–48

About noon the following day as they were on their journey and approaching the city, Peter went up on the roof to pray. [...] He saw heaven opened and something like a large sheet being let down to earth by its four corners. It contained all kinds of four-footed animals, as well as reptiles and birds. Then a voice told him, 'Get up, Peter. Kill and eat.'

'Surely not, Lord!' Peter replied. 'I have never eaten anything impure or unclean.' [...]

While Peter was still thinking about the vision, the Spirit said to him, 'Simon, three men are looking for you. So get up and go downstairs. Do not hesitate to go with them, for I have sent them.' [...]

The next day Peter started out with them, and some of the believers from Joppa went along. The following day he arrived in Caesarea. Cornelius was expecting them and had called together his relatives and close friends. [...] Cornelius answered: 'Three days ago I was in my house praying at this hour, at three in the afternoon. Suddenly a man in shining clothes stood before me and said, "Cornelius, God has heard your prayer and remembered your gifts to the poor. Send to Joppa for Simon who is called Peter. He is a guest in the home of Simon the tanner, who lives by the sea." So I sent for you immediately, and it was good of you to come. Now we are all here in the presence of God to listen to everything the Lord has commanded you to tell us.' Then Peter began to speak: 'I now realise how true it is that God does not show favouritism [...] While Peter was still speaking these words, the Holy Spirit came on all who heard the message. The circumcised believers who had come with Peter were astonished that the gift of the Holy Spirit had been poured out even on Gentiles. For they heard them speaking in tongues and praising God.

Then Peter said, 'Surely no one can stand in the way of their being baptised with water. They have received the Holy Spirit just as we have.' So he ordered that they be baptised in the name of Jesus Christ. Then they asked Peter to stay with them for a few days.

This is a crucial turning point for the newly formed church, which up to this point has been little more than a quirky Jewish sect (note the 'circumcised believers' in verse 45), rejected in Jerusalem and scattered by persecution. Ahead lies one of the biggest potential changes possible: that this message might not be just for the Jews but for Gentiles as well. It is the start of a potentially explosive new growth curve but is, ironically, initially resisted by Peter himself – the very one who has the vision. Later (see Acts 11:18), the believers manage to get their heads around this revolutionary change, and the rest is history.

Exodus 4:18,20–23,27–31

Then Moses went back to Jethro his father-in-law and said to him, 'Let me return to my own people in Egypt to see if any of them are still alive.'

Jethro said, 'Go, and I wish you well.' [...] So Moses took his wife and sons, put them on a donkey and started back to Egypt. And he took the staff of God in his hand.

The LORD said to Moses, 'When you return to Egypt, see that you perform before Pharaoh all the wonders I have given you the power to do. But I will harden his heart so that he will not let the people go. Then say to Pharaoh, "This is what the LORD says: Israel is my firstborn son, and I told you, 'Let my son go, so he may worship me.' But you refused to let him go; so I will kill your firstborn son."' [...] The LORD said to Aaron, 'Go into the wilderness to meet Moses.' So he met Moses at the mountain of God and kissed him. Then Moses told Aaron everything the LORD had sent him to say, and also about all the signs he had commanded him to perform.

Moses and Aaron brought together all the elders of the Israelites, and Aaron told them everything the LORD had said to Moses. He also performed the signs before the people, and they believed. And when they heard that the LORD was concerned about them and had seen their misery, they bowed down and worshipped.

Like many great theories, this one is scalable. God's chosen people are in bondage in Egypt; indeed, it is their numerical growth that has led to reactionary oppression by the Egyptians. A new start means quite literally to break away from the old with all its accompanying risks. Moses is equipped with the ability to demonstrate God's power through miraculous signs but even so, resistance to change is anticipated (v21). A recurring theme in the narrative of Exodus is the people longing for the security of their restricted life in Egypt, whilst trying to trust God that something better is possible. At a human level, the fortunes of God's people may dip before the establishment of their own homeland and security.

And finally...

I have emphasised several times the value in Handy's model in nurturing the courage to change – and change is always a risk.

In 1985, the Coca-Cola corporation reformulated the bestselling soft drink in the world, a change which was considered to be the most memorable marketing blunder ever'.[3] But Coca-Cola were much smarter than people thought – and I'll explain why. Having been steadily losing market share to its main rival for 15 consecutive years, there was little doubt that the curve had peaked. So Coca-Cola pitched their 'new' drink, with the old formula still available in small quantities and labelled 'Classic'. All the marketing effort went into promoting the new formula, which promptly bombed... causing a massive consumer backlash. What Coca-Cola had not allowed for was the *cultural* importance of the drink in many American's lives, and they were seen as tampering with this without being invited to. The new drink lasted exactly 79 days before the original was brought back. Coca-Cola had the luxury of effectively managing to jump back onto their original curve. Paradoxically, the blunder was seen to reinvigorate discussion about the product and remind consumers how important it was to them, leading to a growth in sales. It is now seen as a celebration of allowing employees to take risks and an account of it appears on the company's own website. Hidden in all this is the fact that much of the company's revitalisation was also down to the almost simultaneous launch of Cherry Coke. This was a big success, and represented a much more conventional and sustained example of jumping on to a new curve with a new product.

Coca-Cola (as a company) really have proved to be a sustainable enterprise, and their candid embracing of the story of 'new Coke' is only a small part of a bigger narrative. In more recent times, Coke Zero has been a commercial success. Interestingly, part of this is clearly down to the cultural awareness of new sports drinks, obesity, and a cultural desire for 'healthier' options. The negative experience of 'new Coke' did not lead to paralysis or a refusal to change, but a much greater awareness of cultural nuances and what was required to launch a product successfully.

Author Jim Collins came up with the analogy of 'time tellers' and 'clock builders'. Imagine a world with no clocks – but there are some gifted individuals with the innate ability to tell the time. They are revered for their gift and rise to prominence. Those who are simply time tellers exploit the service they can offer and cash in on it. The clock builders, on the other hand, have the very same gift but are more interested in building long-term productivity around a set of values. Following this analogy, time tellers will be much more relaxed about abandoning a product or service if something better is possible; that is, jumping on to a new product life cycle curve. Clock builders will find this whole process much more challenging because it requires them to reflect on their central *values*, not just products. The advent of new technology (good examples being digital photography, or CDs instead of vinyl) has seen many well-established companies having to make a painful decision between embracing a new and largely unfamiliar process, or shrinking into becoming a niche provider of a now unfashionable product.

I spent seven years working at a theological college. During this time, overall attendance at UK churches (which of course was broadly the 'market' we were serving) continued to decline, so negative growth was a real possibility. In practice, the college was wedded to what I personally called a monastic model of theological formation. Virtually all students were residential in what was a very beautiful if somewhat remote campus. Students were required to do several hours of ministry each week, but there was a real danger of them living and working in a very attractive but removed Christian 'ghetto'. Some of our students had histories of abuse (emotional, physical and substance) so retreating into a strong Christian community for a period was a very therapeutic step. For others however, particularly those from a strong and vibrant Christian background, it may not have been the best option. Eventually, and partially in response to plateauing entry numbers, we launched a new mode of course delivery involving distance learning combined with short but intensive residential teaching weeks. I led the whole project, from getting academic validation and approval, to the practical requirements of the teaching programme. This might sound quite conventional now that we're living in a post-Covid world, but at the time it was somewhat revolutionary. It was fascinating to note the disquiet within the institution – some embracing the new, but others worried that core values (particularly around a hands-on style of spiritual formation) were being abandoned. I remember one conversation with the principal who, in an unguarded moment declared, 'Well, we all know that three years residential at the college is best, but I guess this works for those who can't do that.' I disagreed profoundly. Whilst for some there were barriers of family and finance, for others the distance learning mode offered a *better* learning experience with an apprentice-style approach that enabled learning to be tested out in the workplace very quickly. Ironically, I later came to realise that whilst the choice between residential and distance learning was of course up to the student, in practice, we had residential students who should really have been out in the 'real world' and distance-learning students who could have benefitted from the closer support available to residential students!

I noted earlier the power of asking not 'What do we do?' but 'What are we trying to achieve?' The answer to the first question for us would have been, 'We are running a theology college.' But the much better answer to the second question was, 'We are trying to deliver effective theological training to equip people for ministry.' Once we had got that clear, we were released from just one mode of delivery – no matter how dominant it had been in the past, in tradition and in the history of the organisation.

Handle this with care. What will be evident from the above accounts is that potential change is nearly always difficult, decisive, and painful. As I've said before, the crucial thing about Handy's model is that it gives us the *language* to discuss this; it gives us a set of tools with which to examine what is going on and at least consider the need for radical change. Use the sigmoid curve to strengthen your case for courage and visionary change, but use it with love and compassion.

AFTERWORD

Making links

One of the rules I proposed for this book in the introduction was to try not to link different theories. It's a recipe for confusion when we are trying to grasp and start using some of the tools. Having said that, once we get to grips with the basics, there is a whole new possibility of understanding available by bringing together different insights.

This final chapter is an opportunity to relax that rule, to make some playful connections between different tools and see how one might illuminate or enhance the other. I am also going to introduce different personality typologies and how they might influence how we engage with some tools. I will also touch on some other mainstream thinking that might bring new insights. Linking everything to everything would require a whole new book ,so this is just a small chance to make some creative links – I'm sure you will already have been making some yourself.

Myers-Briggs Type Indicator (MBTI)

Myers-Briggs (named after the mother and daughter team that developed it) is without doubt the most widely known and used personality testing system. Usually administered by qualified MBTI operators, the student fills in an extensive questionnaire, then the numbers are crunched, and the MBTI revealed. MBTI gives and indicator of both preference and strength of preference on four scales, to give 16 possible personality types. The words used have quite specific meanings, so it is important to grasp what is indicated:

Extravert (E) — Introvert (I)
Sensing (S) — INtuition (N)
Thinking (T) — Feeling (F)
Judging (J) — Perceiving (P)

Extraverts are energised by being with other people. They love noise and bustle, conversation, and human company. They love a party but start to feel drained in the car on the way home. Introverts love to work alone, focusing on the task, enjoying their own company. They can tolerate the party but can feel drained at the end and start to feel re-energised in the car on the way home. A standing joke when I worked at a theology college was that extraverts worked in their offices with the door propped open, while introverts worked with it firmly shut!

Sensers focus on facts and details in the here and now. They are great at living in and enjoying the moment. INtuitives focus on possibilities. They find it harder to live in the moment with a greater awareness of other outcomes and possibilities.

Thinkers do what it says on the tin, preferring logical analysis of situations. Feelers are more driven by their own values and relationships that are important to them. A course of action may be logical but if it will upset a friend, they hesitate and find it difficult.

Judgers tend to be organised and, above all, stick to a plan and follow it through regardless. Perceivers are much more open to spontaneous possibilities ('Who knows what today might bring!?') and are happy to change plans in favour of a better option.

So let's start making some links between these personality preferences and some of the tools we've explored.

Think win-win

Imaginative Thinkers will already be making links between this insight and some of the tools we have looked at. Feelers (rather than the logically driven Thinkers) are more likely to intuitively seek a win-win outcome to a transaction, for example. Keeping all parties happy is simply a more natural way of thinking for them.

Time management

In a different context, Judgers and Perceivers are likely to have a very different approach to time management. To be blunt, Judgers are more likely to be able to live in the second box of the 'urgent/important' matrix, sticking to a plan and following through without distractions. In contrast, Perceivers are much more likely to be distracted by what might actually be wonderful and creative opportunities.

Managing conflict

In a similar way, Feelers will find conflict particularly hard. By contrast the Thinkers may be more easily driven by logic to a just outcome, just as iNtuitives and Perceivers may find it easier to imagine a better world that is worth fighting for.

It is important to note that there is never a moral imperative here. We are who we are, created by God is His varied image. No one is better than any other, but awareness of your own tendencies and preferences will help you to grasp which tools you will be able to use easily, and which are going to present more of a challenge to you.

Readers wanting to explore and link win-win thinking and conflict could find the early chapters of David Augsburger's book *Caring Enough to Confront* a rich source of understanding. Augsburger effectively layers win-win thinking on a matrix that plays off concern for *relationship* against concern for *goals*. The resulting chart allows you to plot a different position for different issues in different contexts.[1]

Kotter and Diffusion of Innovation

Kotter's eight-step model of change and Rogers' Diffusion of Innovation are good examples of tools that may (confusingly!) hang together – in some respects, they might be flipsides to each other. Kotter identifies the need to find a coalition to drive change – these are likely to be Rogers' innovators and early adopters. These are the people who will naturally create vision for change and communicate it (steps 3 and 4). MBTI's iNtuitives and Perceivers will again have an advantage in imagining change and promoting it. Sensers will struggle. Everett's late majority and laggards are the ones who will struggle most both with the vision for change but also adapting and adopting culturally new working practices. We don't need to try to link the two theories, but each can complement and enhance the other, bringing deeper insights.

Kubler-Ross

There is also a potentially strong link between both Kotter's eight-step change theory, diffusion of innovation and the well-known theory on death and dying proposed by Elizabeth Kubler-Ross. Drawing on a huge range of experience of work with the dying, Kubler-Ross proposed five stages of grief: denial, anger, bargaining, depression, and acceptance. Kubler-Ross's theory is a classic in that whilst many professionals would consider it simplistic, rigid, and now superseded by others, it continues to have a powerful hold in the public's imagination and is still well known and referred to. Whilst built on the experience of those who were literally dying, it is often used by observers to explain the behaviour of others facing any sort of loss. Inasmuch as significant change involves loss, it may well bring huge insight to the process of change and naturally complements both Kotter and diffusion of innovation. Leaders with some familiarity with Kubler-Ross may be able to recognise some of the reactions exhibited by people in the face of change and potential (or actual) loss.

Engel and Everett

In Christian ministry, Engel's scale has been a mainstay theory for over forty years. Engel's key insight was that most people no longer make a step of faith on hearing the gospel message but embark on a much longer process of incremental steps towards a decision. I note this because Engel's steps have an uncanny resemblance to Rogers' observations on how individuals adopt a new idea. I am not inferring plagiarism here, simply that great minds think alike! Likewise, diffusion of innovation has a lot to teach us in terms of our wider evangelistic strategy.

SWOT

The ease with which a person can navigate the different sections of SWOT will again be significantly impacted by personality type. MBTI Sensers will probably have a heightened sense of threats but struggle with visualising opportunities (which iNtuitives will easily be able to spot). Perceivers will be the diametric opposite of this! Some threats may be wicked problems and thwart a potentially positive SWOT experience. Likewise, A Belbin Plant or Resource Investigator will be able to perceive opportunities that a Monitor Evaluator simply can't imagine; meanwhile, if the organisation is a power culture (Handy), the leader will be wondering why they ever agreed to a SWOT exercise, as it is obvious they know best anyway.

Tuckman

The gem in Tuckman's group theory is the paradoxical observation that groups need a 'storming' period of conflict before settling down to a high level of performance. We noted the role of the leader in this process: fairly hands-on in the early stages but potentially more hands-off in the latter stages. There is a clear link between Tuckman and the conflict curve: if conflict is inevitable at stage two of Tuckman but must be worked through, any leader equipped with an insight into the trajectory that conflict is likely to take has an advantage. As an observation, most groups or teams are very unlikely to reach the highest levels of conflict, but that does not negate the advantage of understanding the bigger picture. The leader's role in developing the group is first to recognise the prospect of conflict – indeed, to engender a sense of security where robust conflict is 'safe' enough to happen. Leaders can set rules for conflict where, despite differences, people feel safe to express an opinion and know that it has been heard. Managing this well may then set a precedent for the inevitable future conflicts that will arise – remember that 'storming' will inevitably be returned to as changes take place in some aspect of the group's life.

In terms of MBTI, Thinkers may find it easier to lead a group through this than Feelers, who have a heightened sensitivity to the pain of conflict.

Belbin

Team builders have everything to gain from the observations already made around Tuckman and groups. Good teams also have an interesting and deeply philosophical aspect. In *Falling Upwards*, Richard Rohr[2] analyses the 'two halves' of life and makes a vital observation. Many of the qualities that we use in the first half of life (when we generally build our careers), such as competitiveness and independence, do not serve us well in the second half. It is a 'second half of life' observation to see interdependence (a crucial quality of great teams) as a higher goal than independence, or being the 'star' of a team. David Gilmour, the master of the extended guitar solo and front man for rock band Pink Floyd was asked in 2020 what his favourite Pink Floyd song was. In a moment of beautiful irony, he replied *'Echoes*, I always look on that song as being very much a duet thing between [Richard Wright] and me.'[3] There is something beautiful about someone most famous for their solos appreciating the interdependence of a duet.

Handy's organisational culture

Handy's insights cry out to be connected with decision-making processes. A genuine role culture, for example, is very likely to embrace SWOT as a way of making rational (and defensible) decisions. A power culture may pay lip service to SWOT but is more likely to ride roughshod over it whilst the leader makes decisions. A role culture may be slow to perceive the need for change but will embrace Kotter's plan when change is required; it is a logical, corporate way of managing the situation that resonates nicely with role culture thinking. We noted in the chapter on Belbin the danger of our human tendency to 'recruit in our own image' when great teams must feature great diversity. A task culture can be particularly strong here as the very nature of the organisation may well call for a varied team.

Functional leadership

Team building is a major preoccupation for functional leaders so they will be wise to draw heavily on both conflict resolution and Belbin's model of teams.

Situational leadership

The 'telling and selling' style of leadership that is required with low-skill or low-motivation workers, is by definition more hands-on and directive; more focused on changing the way someone works. As such, situational leaders will find themselves connecting with many other tools. Workers may be slow to change not because they are belligerently resistant but because they are slow adopters – perhaps they simply don't get or trust the new tasks and systems that we are asking them to work with. Likewise, perhaps they have a role on a team that is inconsistent with their Belbin persona.

Situational leadership, as noted in the chapter, really is one of the most challenging roles in the book. As such, leaders will need to draw on a whole range of tools. What is urgent and what is important? How do we manage change as we take an organisation forward? How do we emotionally engage those whose approach is clinical and dispassionate?

And finally...

David and Clare Hieatt are successful serial entrepreneurs who founded Hiut Denim in 2012, a company that has bucked fashion trends by successfully and sustainably manufacturing jeans in the UK when most clothes manufacture is done with very questionable ethics in Asia. One of their founding values is: 'Do one thing well'.[4]

I noted the danger of only having one tool in the box (if we have a hammer, everything looks like a nail), but we can *start* with only one tool. If this type of thinking is new to you, pick one or two tools and self-consciously practise using them. Introduce them to your team and bounce ideas off each other. What you will find is that, as you begin to grasp one tool well, you will find it easier and faster to grasp others, until working with tools becomes an instinctive and natural skill.

James 1:23–24 says: 'For anyone who hears the word but does not carry it out is like a man who looks at his face in a mirror, and after observing himself goes away and immediately forgets what he looks like.' This doesn't sound like a big deal until you consider no one in his culture had modern, silvered mirrors. To see even a version of your reflection involved staring into water (like Narcissus) or polished metal. Social psychologists tell us that it takes an average of about two months for a new habit to become truly ingrained. Remember, that is an average. I once did a training session for some youth workers, and we covered Covey's urgent/important matrix. The following week I coincidentally found myself in a phone conversation with one of the participants. 'Was that bit helpful?' I asked. 'Oh yes!' came the reply, 'I have taped the handout to the desk next to my phone.' This is brilliant psychology. Like James' listeners, it is easy to 'see' or grasp a new theory; it is much, much harder to make it an ingrained, natural part of our thinking. The easiest option is to forget it and go back to our normal ways of thinking and operating.

The best theories in our toolbox can become such a natural part of our outlook that they eventually become part of our world-view – the very lenses through which we observe and make sense of our world. C.S. Lewis famously said: 'I believe in Christianity as I believe that the Sun has risen not only because I see it but because by it I see everything else.'[5] – a brilliantly concise expression of what a world-view is.

There is an extraordinary example of this in the Old Testament. The Israelites are about to cross the Jordan into the Promised Land and Moses, painfully aware of their resistance to their new status as God's chosen people, briefs them: 'These commandments that I give you today are to be on your hearts. Impress them on your children. Talk about them when you sit at home and when you walk along the road, when you lie down and when you get up. Tie them as symbols on your hands and bind them on your foreheads. Write them on the doorframes of your houses and on your gates' (Deut. 6:6–9). This is Moses' version of 'taping it to the desk'. God's people had repeatedly shown their ability to stick with old ways of thinking and worship, and Moses recognises the need to actively working at changing their thinking. Modern psychology in the Old Testament – who knew?

My hope is that with practice, some of these tools will become part of your own worldview – the natural way by which you make sense of what is happening around you. This book will help you grasp the theories but, like learning a new sporting technique, you must intentionally practise – a lot.

These tools have blessed me, and I invite you to let them bless you.

ENDNOTES

Introduction

[1] M. Scott Peck, *The Road Less Travelled: Classic Editions* (London: Penguin Random House, 2021) p1

[2] Abraham Harold Maslow, *The Psychology of Science: A Reconnaissance* (New York: Harper and Row, 1966). Maslow did say this in his book but, like so many famous quotes, there is significant evidence that he may have been drawing on the earlier sayings of others in this field, in this case Abraham Kaplan.

[3] Lucy Denyer, 'Stephen Cottrell: 'Cut the Church some slack – it's incredible what we do', 2 April 2021, taken from telegraph.co.uk (Accessed January 2023)

[4] Richard R. Rohr, *The Enneagram: A Christian Perspective* (New York: Crossroad, 2018)

[5] I say 'widely quoted' because although this wisdom appears on hundreds of management and leadership sites, what Peter Drucker actually said was: 'Efficiency is concerned with doing things right. Effectiveness is doing the right things.' This can be found in Peter Drucker, *People and Performance* (Abingdon-on-Thames: Routledge, 1995).

[6] A transcript of this interview with Bill Moyers of PBS (conducted on 27 April, 1999) can be found at pbs.org/moyers/journal/12282007/watch2.html (Accessed January 2023)

[7] John O'Donohue, *Anam Cara* (New York: Bantam Books, 1997) p13

Chapter 1

[1] Ronald Regan's' 1977 interview with Richard Allen for an article titled, 'The man who won the cold war', available at hoover.org (Accessed January 2023)

[2] Stephen Covey, *7 Habits of Highly Effective People* (New York: Simon & Schuster, 2020)

[3] David Augsburger, *Caring Enough to Confront* (London: Regal, 2009) p23

Chapter 2

[1] David Augsberger, *Ibid*, p11

[2] M. Lund, *Preventing Violent Conflicts: A Strategy for Preventive Diplomacy* (Washington DC: Institute for Peace Press, 1996)

[3] Archbishop Desmond Tutu is powerfully quoted in Bono's *Surrender* (London: Hutchinson, 2022) p452

Chapter 3

[1] This was printed in a booklet called *Tyranny of the Urgent*, written by Charles Hummel and published by IVP in 1994. Various editions are still available online. Hummel's thinking was later written up in the subsequent *Freedom from the Tyranny of the Urgent*, also published by IVP in 1994.

[2] Dr Dion Klein, 'Urgency Addiction: The New Corporate Disease' (2 July 2019), found at wellness.edu.au (Accessed January 2023)

Chapter 4

[1] This quote is widely attributed to Churchill. Richard Langworth, in his book *Churchill by Himself*, traces it to a speech in the House of Commons on 23 June 1925, although it seems Churchill was actually quoting Cardinal John Henry Newman's *Essays on the Development of Christian Doctrine*. Churchill may of course have assumed people were familiar with the cultural reference he was making.

[2] Ronald A. Heifetz, Marty Linsky and Alexander Grashow, *Adaptive Leadership: The Heifetz Collection* (Boston, MA, USA: Harvard Business Review Press, 2014) p185

[3]Stephen Covey, *The 7 Habits of Highly Effective Families* (New York: Simon & Schuster, 1998), p72

[4]Deal and Kennedy, *Corporate Cultures: The Rites and Rituals of Corporate Life* (New York: Basic Books, 1982)

[5]John Kotter, *Leading Change* (Boston, MA, USA: Harvard Business Review Press, 2012)

Chapter 5

[1]Bono, *Ibid*, p431

[2]Elihu Katz and Paul F. Lazarsfeld, *Personal Influence* (New York: Free Press, 1957)

Chapter 6

[1]Taken from a social media post by Greta Thunberg on Twitter (@GretaThunberg), 31 August 2019 (Post still accessible as of January 2023)

[2]Niccolo Machiavelli, *The Prince* (originally published in 1532)

[3]*Fortune* magazine claims to be the originator of this phrase, under the authorship of William White Jr in 1952. White's thesis was simply that positive adoption of consensus within a group can lead to the rapid rejection of other valid ideas and approaches. What looks like great decision making may in fact be the group talking itself into disaster.

Chapter 7

[1]Albert Einstein, quoted in the *New York Times*, 25 May 1946

[2]David Gibson, *Living Life Backwards* (Wheaton, IL, USA: Crossway, 2017) p82

[3]'Wesleyan holiness': the belief that complete sanctification (the eradication of all sin) is possible.

Chapter 8

[1]Like numerous famous quotes, the veracity of the attribution to Margaret Mead is not easy to pin down. I found this cited in Donald Keys, *Earth at Omega: Passage to Planetization* (Boston, MA, USA: Branden Press, 1982)

[2]Note that this spelling of 'Extravert' is the most commonly found in psychological writing.

Chapter 9

[1]Dr Raymond Meredith Belbin, *Management Teams* (Portsmouth: NH, USA: Butterworth, Heinemann, 1981) p ix

[2]See Covey, *The 7 Habits of Highly Effective Families*, *Ibidi*, p389, where my edition shows a the diagram of the seven habits. Interdependence is a recurring theme and an aim of the entire book.

[3]You can download a PDF For Students here: https://www.belbin.com/media/1336/belbin-for-students.pdf (Accessed January 2023), and go to page 13.

[4]See either Belbin's original book (see note above), which has a self-perception inventory test which can be self-administered, or see https://www.belbin.com/about/belbin-team-roles (accessed January 2023). This is The Belbin Organisation's own site and allows the purchase of online tests for yourself or your whole team.

Chapter 10

[1]This quote is almost universally attributed to Drucker (who died in November 2005), although pinning down when and where is tricky. It was used by Mark Field, a later CEO of the Ford Motor Company, in 2006 – according to an Associated Press report on the car manufacturer, this quote was one of a number of slogans written on the wall of the company's conference room.

Chapter 11

[1]Max Hastings, *Abyss: The Cuban Missile Crisis* (Glasgow: William Collins, 2022) p116

[2]SMART is an industry standard acronym. Objectives need to be Specific, Measurable, Achievable, Realistic (or Relevant) and Timebound. SMART is a leadership tool to avoid vague and generalised

ambitions being talked about in an unrealistic way.

[3]J. Adair, *Action Centred Leadership* (Aldershot, UK: Gower, 1979)

Chapter 12

[1]J. O'Donohue, *Ibid*, p118

Chapter 13

[1]Winston Churchill, widely cited in a variety of sources.

[2]J.M. Burns, *Leadership* (New York: Harper and Row, 1978) p20

[3]Bono, *Ibid*, p422

[4]Dietrich Bonhoeffer, *The Cost of Discipleship* (London: SCM Press, 1948/2001) p44

[5]Robert Lawrence, *When the Fighting is Over* (London: Bloomsbury, 1988)

Chapter 14

[1]Robert Harris, *Dictator* (London: Hutchinson, 2015)

[2]Various streaming sites still show episodes of *Tim Allen Rewires America*, c1991.

[3]This story is now widely celebrated by Coca-Cola and you can read about it on their website: coca-colacompany.com/company/history (Accessed January 2023)

Afterword

[1]David Augsburger, *ibid*, p19

[2]Richard Rohr, *Falling Upwards* (London: SPCK, 2013)

[3]*Far Out* magazine, May 2022 – see faroutmagazine.co.uk

[4]You can read more about this at hiutdenim.co.uk/blogs/our-story (Accessed January 2023)

[5]C.S. Lewis, 'They Asked For A Paper,' in *Is Theology Poetry?*" (London: Geoffrey Bless, 1962), 164-165

WAVERLEY ABBEY
COLLEGE

Develop your gifts • Be equipped • Make a difference

Equipping people to be the positive impact on society through courses in:

- **Counselling**
- **Spiritual Formation**
- **Contemporary courses in Chaplaincy, Discipleship and Church Ministry**

waverleyabbeycollege.ac.uk

A hub of spiritual encounter, Christian education, innovative enterprise and community engagement.

Waverley Abbey Trust is a ministry, equipping you to love God, love your neighbour and love yourself.

Through our portfolio of courses and resources, you can learn to be the difference in society.

Find out more today.

waverleyabbeytrust.org